CW00924977

Unlock
Group Potential
to Improve Schools

Unlocking
Group Potential
to Improve Schools

Robert J. Garmston with Valerie von Frank

Foreword by Michael Fullan

CORWIN
A SAGE Company

CORWIN
A SAGE Company

FOR INFORMATION

Corwin
A SAGE Company
2455 Teller Road
Thousand Oaks, California 91320
(800) 233-9936
www.corwin.com

SAGE Publications Ltd.
1 Oliver's Yard
55 City Road
London, EC1Y 1SP
United Kingdom

SAGE Publications India Pvt. Ltd.
B 1/I 1 Mohan Cooperative Industrial Area
Mathura Road, New Delhi
India 110 044

SAGE Publications Asia-Pacific Pte. Ltd.
3 Church Street
#10-04 Samsung Hub
Singapore 049483

Acquisitions Editor: Arnis Burvikovs
Associate Editor: Desirée A. Bartlett
Editorial Assistant: Kimberly Greenberg
Production Editor: Amy Schroller
Copy Editor: Alan Cook
Typesetter: Hurix Systems Pvt. Ltd
Proofreader: Eleni-Maria Georgiou
Indexer: Sylvia Coates
Cover Designer: Karine Hovsepian
Permissions Editor: Karen Ehrman

Printed in the United States of America

Library of Congress Cataloging-in-Publication Data

Garmston, Robert J.

Unlocking group potential to improve schools / Robert J. Garmston with Valerie von Frank.

pages cm

Includes bibliographical references and index.

ISBN 978-1-4129-9889-5 (pbk.)

1. Group work in education. 2. Professional learning communities. 3. Educational change. 4. School improvement programs. I. Von Frank, Valerie. II. Title.

LB1032.G38 2013

371.39'5—dc23

2012007492

This book is printed on acid-free paper.

SUSTAINABLE FORESTRY INITIATIVE

Certified Chain of Custody
Promoting Sustainable Forestry
www.sfiprogram.org
SFI-01268

SFI label applies to text stock

12 13 14 15 16 10 9 8 7 6 5 4 3 2 1

Contents

SECTION IV: Developing Facilitation Skills

Foreword

Getting work done in groups is a paradox. It should be so easy—common sense, one could say. Yet history's most fundamental blunders are a result of groups gone awry. Whether it is a world crisis or getting through the day, knowing how to behave in groups, how to lead them, and how to facilitate them is one of life's fundamental skills.

Fortunately we have Bob Garmston, who has led the cognitive coaching field for several decades. He is a writer and a practitioner—a trainer and a consultant. He has also been distilling his wisdom in regular columns in the publications of the National Staff Development Council (NSDC; now Learning Forward). Now, with Valerie von Frank, Garmston has brought together in one publication systematic and honed wisdom in the fundamentals of group work and group management.

Garmston first tackles the matter of "getting work done," delving into understanding and building effective groups. He then takes us into developing group member skills. From there we learn how to develop a sense of community, including how to become self-directed. The final section addresses facilitation skills that will be essential for intervening and maintaining effective group work.

What makes *Unlocking Group Potential to Improve Schools* special is that it easily cycles back and forth from deep issues and skills of effective group functioning to the seemingly most mundane but nonetheless critical basics of setting up a room, organizing the agenda, conducting sessions, and so on.

What is great about this book is that it contains the complete package, ranging from operating norms to micro and macro skills, leadership, and facilitation. The reader does not have to go hunting through the literature in order to identify and sort out the skills of group work. Take this one book, master its content, practice its principles and techniques, refine your knowledge and skill base, and watch yourself and your group get better and better. This is a book that keeps on giving. Read and reread it, practice its tenets, and you and those you work with will be much better off. Unlock your potential!

Michael Fullan, Professor Emeritus
Ontario Institute for Studies in Education
University of Toronto

Preface

Why Read This Book?

This book is about developing group culture, increasing facilitator knowledge and skill, and developing the most precious resource groups have—the members themselves. In short, this book is about leadership for better schools—schools that are better for students, better places for leaders to grow as learners, and better environments for inquiry.

The book can be considered a field guide for two reasons. First, it is written based on my interactions with many groups in the field; second, because the original form of much of the content came in columns, the ideas presented are specific and practical, but not without theoretical foundation. It was inspired by more than 40 years of working with groups on several continents and the resulting columns I wrote for the *Journal of Staff Development,* a publication of the National Staff Development Council, now named Learning Forward. In those columns, I developed many specific ideas that I lay before you now.

The tools, tips, and principles I present here will make working committees, task forces, and grade-level and department teams and faculties not only more effective and efficient, but smarter and able to resolve cognitively complex issues regarding student learning more effectively. Readers also will learn to discern which problems may be solved and which are ongoing tensions that need to be managed.

Who Is This Book For?

Productive groups are developed, not born. This book is a developmental field book for all those laboring in schools and seeking collective improvement in student learning. It is written for anyone needing a current, practical guide to group work.

Here, readers will find not only what makes effective teams, but how to develop teacher skills as facilitators and informed group members in informal and formal settings, small groups and large.

The book takes readers beyond the idea of *professional learning communities* to the practice, describing specific ways to weave the collaborative fabric of a faculty, develop group member skills, and improve facilitation strategies. District and building administrators, K–12 teachers, university students, and teacher leaders of all types—mentors, coaches, and committee and department chairs—will find it useful for working with staffs, parents, or communities.

What's New About This Book?

In *The Adaptive School* (2009), Bruce Wellman and I describe how professional development and ongoing focus on developing the system as an adaptive entity can help groups develop their capacity for productivity. In this book I extend, add depth, provide how-tos, provide more detail about the principles, and bring together more tools and tips for unlocking group potential. The structure of the book should make the material easily accessible to groups, from novice to veteran.

Readers will learn to work together more effectively. This book contains the most current research, revisions to the norms of collaboration and related assessment instruments, and detailed instructions for facilitating and intervening with counterproductive individuals or group behaviors.

A focus on collective intelligence enhances my previous work and provides information to guide readers through the latest research on the concept, what factors are involved, and how to increase collective IQ, leading to the ability to solve increasingly complex issues.

Special Features

Special features of this book include the newly updated seven norms of collaboration, a sample team assessment survey, instruments for assessing meeting effectiveness, an extensive bibliography, and practical examples and suggestions embedded throughout the text.

Readers who use this text will be better able to

- Develop productive, collaborative work cultures,
- Improve collective focus on student learning, and
- Acquire the principles and understanding to engage in a continuous cycle of self-improvement.

Acknowledgments

I am massively indebted to Valerie von Frank, without whose assistance this book would not have been possible. Valerie and I worked together as editor and author for several years when I was writing columns for the *Journal of Staff Development*. On contemplating this volume, I thought first of her amazing skills of research, organization, and editing and asked her to join me in this enterprise. Thankfully, she said yes, and the result is the book you hold in your hands. I appreciate Learning Forward, formerly the National Staff Development Council, for giving me a forum to develop some of these ideas in my columns for the journal.

Many people contributed to the ideas in this book. I am grateful to Bruce Wellman, a partner in the development of the Center for Adaptive Schools and several publications; his thinking and creativity are always at the forefront of our profession. I thank Michael Dolcemascolo and Carolyn McKanders, codirectors of the Center for Adaptive Schools which has served as a testing ground and training vehicle for many of the concepts I've elaborated on here. They have advanced this work while remaining true to its principles and values and given permission for some of the content in this book. For deepening our understanding and adding to this work, I thank Jane Ellison and Carolee Hayes, codirectors of the Center for Cognitive Coaching. And my appreciation goes to Bill and Ochan Powell, who practice and teach this content internationally and from whom I always learn.

A big "Thank you" is due to Mylene Keipp, a response to instruction and intervention coordinator in the Los Angeles Unified Schools District Local District 5. She gave me valuable feedback to portions of the text and tirelessly sought and provided stories from colleagues illustrating portions of this work. A thank you as well, to Frances Gipson, administrator of instruction for Local District 5, who provides inspired leadership and makes a difference in schools with challenging circumstances. She consistently keeps the focus on kids and poses the relevant and tough questions to teachers and administrators. From Frances, we all have learned a lot.

Mark Ravlin, at my request, revised and gave permission for me to use the Seven Norms of Collaboration Toolkit, available to readers in the Appendixes of this book, and on www.adaptiveschools.com. I am also thankful to the principal, Liliana Narvaez, and teachers of the Estrella School— a Garmston and Costa Academy, who contribute to our knowledge base through their daily practice of the principles and tools of Adaptive Schools, Cognitive Coaching, and Habits of Mind.

Finally, I am grateful for the legions of Adaptive Schools colleagues who both train others and practice these skills in their own settings. We are, ourselves, a community of learners.

Robert Garmston
El Dorado Hills, California

PUBLISHER'S ACKNOWLEDGMENTS

Corwin would like to thank the following individuals for taking the time to provide their editorial insight:

Roberta E. Glaser
Retired Assistant Superintendent
St. Johns Public Schools
St. Johns, Missouri

Kathy Grover
Assistant Superintendent
Clever R-V Public Schools
Clever, Montana

Douglas Gordon Hesbol
Superintendent
Laraway Community Consolidated School District 70C
Joliet, Illinois

Scott Hollinger
Executive Coach
Communities Foundation of Texas/Texas High School Project
Dallas, Texas

Pamela Maxwell
Principal
Kennedy Elementary School
Peace River, Alberta, Canada

Roberto Pamas
Principal
O.W. Holmes Middle School
Alexandria, Virginia

About the Authors

 **Robert J. Garmston, EdD**, is an Emeritus Professor of Educational Administration at California State University, Sacramento and codeveloper of Cognitive Coaching (www.cognitivecoaching.com) with Dr. Art Costa. Formerly a classroom teacher, principal, director of instruction, and acting superintendent, he works as an educational consultant and is director of Facilitation Associates, a consulting firm specializing in leadership, learning, personal, and organizational development. He is codeveloper of the Center for Adaptive Schools (www.adaptiveschools.com) with Bruce Wellman. The Center for Adaptive Schools develops organizational capacity for self-directed, sustainable improvement in student learning. He has made presentations and conducted workshops for teachers, administrators, and staff developers throughout the United States, as well as in Canada, Africa, Asia, Australia, Europe, and the Middle East.

Bob has written and coauthored a number of books including *Cognitive Coaching: A Foundation for Renaissance Schools*, *How to Make Presentations That Teach and Transform*, and *A Presenter's Fieldbook: A Practical Guide*. In 1999, the National Staff Development Council (NSDC) selected *The Adaptive School: A Sourcebook for Developing Collaborative Groups* as book of the year. In that same year, Bob was recognized by NSDC for his contributions to staff development. His books have been translated into Arabic, Hebrew, and Italian.

Active in many professional organizations, Bob served as president of the California Association for Supervision and Curriculum Development and as a member of the Executive Council of the Association for Supervision and Curriculum Development (ASCD) at the international level. In addition to educational clients, he has worked with diverse groups including police officers, probation officers, court and justice systems, utilities districts, the United States Air Force, and the World Health Organization.

Bob lives with his wife, Sue, near Sacramento, California and has five children and five grandchildren, each of whom, of course, is bright and cute.

Valerie von Frank has had a front row seat on education reform in the past several decades. As a daily newspaper reporter and editor in multiple states, communications co-director in an urban school district, and director of communications for a nonprofit school reform organization, she has explored with educators the multiple facets of daily work in schools. In the last decade, she has worked with Learning Forward as editor of *JSD* and written extensively for the journal, as well as for *Tools for Schools, The Learning System, The Learning Principal,* and *T3*. She is co-author with Ann Delehant of *Making Meetings Work: How to Get Started, Get Going, and Get It Done* (Corwin, 2007) and with Linda Munger of *Change, Lead, Succeed: Building Capacity With School Leadership Teams* (NSDC, 2010).

She currently lives in Michigan, where her two daughters receive an excellent public education.

Introduction

National improvement on standardized tests seems a goal just out of reach. The lack of improvement in overall school performance is evident both in the research literature and in the media (Good & McCaslin, 2008). But this is not the full story. In Illinois, California, and Nebraska; in Hawaii, Ohio, and Idaho; in New York, Calgary, and many other settings, urban and rural, rich and poor, some schools are making a difference for students. The difference is measured in unusual progress on standardized tests, improved attendance, higher graduation rates, and the exuberant smiles of students being pressed and supported in their learning and play.

What dynamics have enabled some schools to become these islands of optimism? The answers are neither simple nor easy. For schools to succeed in improving student learning requires leaders' attention to a mutually supportive, multilayered, nonlinear, extraordinarily complex, often competitive association of interrelated factors (National Commission on Teaching and America's Future, 2010). In these schools are teams of teachers with shared values and goals, able to clearly identify a problem and come together to improve student learning. These teams share a collective sense of responsibility and accountability for student achievement. Teachers use authentic assessments as essential tools to improve learning. They practice self-directed reflection based on their own and student needs. The schools are stable settings—collaborative work cannot occur in dysfunctional environments. These are schools in which strong leaders build cultures of openness and trust, empower teams to make decisions that improve student learning, and apply pressure when necessary.

Improving curriculum, often in the face of overwhelming difficulties, remains a central goal in improving schools. Yet, as Kruse and Louis (2009) assert, leaders of moving schools are stretching past the immediate pressure to focus just on curriculum. They also concentrate on integrating the fragmented subcultures that exist in every school as a means to improving instruction, and thus, achievement. These leaders create a vision of what the school might be, offer encouragement, obtain resources, provide constant feedback, and monitor improvement. Groups at many system levels bring together the elements that produce student learning and a culture of shared work. In moving schools, collaboration is a key to success.

It has become self-evident that schools in which faculty members feel a collective responsibility for student learning produce greater learning gains than do schools in which teachers work as isolated practitioners (Louis, Marks, & Kruse, 1996). Louis's research found school-based, professional communities have greater potential to create teacher empowerment, personal dignity, and collective responsibility for student learning. Work on collective efficacy (Goddard, Hoy, & Woolfolk, 2000), on academic optimism, (Hoy, Tarter, & Hoy, 2006), and trust (Bryk & Schneider, 2004; Forsyth, Adams, & Hoy, 2011; Tschannen-Moran, 2004) are adjunct to and extend Louis' findings.

I propose that to develop world-class educational systems—school by school—we learn from this research and focus on creating cultures in schools that foster the development of groups capable of creating rich and sustained student achievement. Working with culture is efficient; changes in culture impact sets of teachers, not just one teacher at a time. In this book, I define principles and practices of group work that have been demonstrated to be effective in a wide range of settings. Leadership practices in schools that support and reinforce accountable cultures make a difference in student learning.

I argue that an important goal of leadership and professional development is to create a culture in which the potential of groups and the individuals involved is unleashed for the betterment of our students.

Expert groups are made, not born. In moving schools, in contrast to stuck schools, working groups grow, develop, learn from experience, and become smarter and more effective at their work. In less effective schools, things stay the same, the group's learning is episodic and disjointed, and members' capacity to work together and teach may remain relatively static.

All groups work at less than full potential. The best groups regard this fact not as a deficiency, but as a healthy dissatisfaction with current performance. They consistently commit resources to working more effectively. Research teams get better with experience, baseball teams practice, and theater casts review their last performance. All groups improve at their tasks when they reflect on their work, acquire new knowledge and skills, and practice the fundamentals of their craft.

Underlying discussion about collaborative teams that impact student learning are several realities. First, each group is unique. The group's history, members' cognitive styles, the school setting, individuals' mental models, and the group's tasks each contribute to a group personality. Each group is not only unlike other groups but different from the sum of the individuals comprising the group. These differences can occur within a single school. For example, the English chair in one high school I know brokered, magnified, and leveraged district resources to benefit professional learning for teachers within that department. The social studies teaching team, with an external locus of control, had none of the same resources.

Some groups mature. Some mature along a continuum from novice toward expert performance. But not all groups make this journey, just as not all teachers achieve the level of expert. Researcher David Berliner (1988) speculated that the novice stage in teaching might last 1 year and that most teachers would reach the third stage (competence) in 3 or 4 years.

Only a modest proportion of teachers move to the next stage of proficiency, and even fewer, he said, to the expert stage. The same seems to be true of group development.

Reflection, it turns out, is key to growth. A dilemma dogs each group. In practically every meeting, working groups have more tasks than time. While it seems logical to invest all available meeting time in working, doing so results in negligible learning about how to work most effectively and little likelihood that the group will progress to the next stages of maturity. This universal truth holds: Any group too busy to reflect about its work is too busy to improve. Effective teams are conscious of what makes them effective. They possess knowledge about being a productive group.

Because so much of professional work occurs during meetings, teams must consider how to ensure that meetings are successful. For more than 20 years, my colleagues and I at the Center for Adaptive Schools have been amazed at how applying eight principles has liberated leaders and faculties to have more productive and satisfying meetings. While we have not articulated them before, it's my sense that these principles should be baseline knowledge for all groups and are important enough to be taught in leadership courses, as well as courses in curriculum development and school finance. The principles that follow are not rules and are subject to a group's wise adaptation to meet members' circumstances. Adapting these principles before applying them, however, is counterproductive and tends to leave groups with faulty premises and tools. The wheel has already been developed. Use it.

EIGHT PRINCIPLES ON WHICH THIS BOOK IS BASED

1. Social capital is important. Research finds that groups are smarter when members have social sensitivity and turn-taking norms, and that they are more successful when there is more positivity than negativity, more inquiry than advocacy, and more focus on others than on self (Losada & Heaphy, 2004; Woolley, Chabris, Pentland, Hashmi, & Malone, 2010).

When groups learn sound norms of group behavior, their levels of group understanding deepen, and shared account-ability for thinking and doing increases. The group moves toward unconscious competence and heightened inquiry. As a result, for example, when given a daunting task like allocat-ing $20,000 before the end of the week, a skillful group resists the urge to mindlessly brainstorm possibilities and instead attends to ways of talking that lead to thoughtful, data-based decisions.

Groups in which members attend to others' social mes-sages are better able to solve cognitively complex prob-lems than groups in which the social messages are mixed. Simultaneous levels operate in any communication. When the social level message (usually in words) says one thing and the psychological message (usually reflected in voice tone, use of gesture, or emphasis) indicates something else, the psycho-logical message, outside of awareness, will be the determinant of the outcome (Lankton & Lankton, 1983).

This is why the seven norms of collaboration described in Chapter 6, with their nonverbal components, are such a powerful resource for groups. It is also why facilitator trust and rapport with a group is so important and why facilitators' nonverbal skills are as important, if not more so, than verbal skills.

2. The quality of a facilitator matters; the quality of the group matters more (Garmston & Wellman, 2009). Workplace culture informs what teachers do more than their skills, edu-cation, or experience do (Frymier, 1987; Kruse & Louis, 2009; Rosenholtz, 1989). This principle is the reason we must work to develop groups, not just facilitators. The best facilitator in the world is unable to help members of a group unwilling to work together to achieve successes. A more modestly skilled facili-tator, on the other hand, can achieve successes with a group whose members are willing to adjust their personal and col-lective goals to achieve an end. The more knowledge members have about how to work as a group, the greater success they can have, even without outside facilitation. Chapter 2 describes the role of a *citizen facilitator*, a member of a small team who both facilitates and contributes to the group's deliberations.

Developing skills as a group member is essential. Since behavior stems from inner drives, skillful group members must have self-awareness and self-monitoring skills to be the best advocates for students that they can be. Self-awareness and self-monitoring require a metacognitive array of skills explored in this book.

3. Groups move toward expediency. *Satisfice* is a word coined by Herbert Simon (Simon, 1982). The word blends *satisfy* with *suffice*. Satisficing means accepting what is satisfactory rather than working to find the best possible outcome; it is a decision-making mindset that seeks a good enough, although not necessarily perfect, course of action. Making a *satisficient* decision means comparing a few alternatives and choosing the best course from this limited range of options.

Simon pointed out that human beings lack the cognitive resources to consider the potential outcomes of all options. So we take shortcuts and accept options that seem to satisfy the criteria of "good enough."

Satisficing is part of the human condition, reports Gary Klein in *Sources of Power: How People Make Decisions* (1999). Klein studied naturalistic decision making: how people make high-stakes decisions in real settings with time pressure, vague goals, limited information, and changing conditions.

Klein's team of observers studied field commanders at fire scenes with the generally accepted model of rational decision-making: faced with a problem, a person gathers information, identifies the possible solutions, and chooses the best one. As it turned out, the fire commanders didn't compare *any* options. They took the first reasonable plan that came to mind and did a quick mental test for problems. If they didn't find any, they had their plan of action (Syed, 2010).

Group members need to recognize when satisficing is not providing an optimal solution, and facilitators should press groups to look beyond the first easy answer.

Related to the idea of satisficence is a human tendency to work on what is urgent rather than what is important. Teachers, like administrators, are often beset with figurative fires to extinguish. If they remain inflexible, they become firemen and lose leadership capacity. To counter this tendency, a principal in Sunnyvale, California, preempted the problem. He gathered key staff around him—secretaries, a resource teacher, a special education teacher, and a mentor teacher. The group defined "an emergency" and discovered the principal was not essential to resolving most of the crises that appeared on their list. This principal's flexibility came from his sense of identity. Rather than being a fireman, he believed himself to be an instructional leader and organized resources around him so he could behave like one. We explore this principle in Chapters 3 and 7.

4. People make the best choices available to them. Human nature is quick to make judgments, and the brain is wired to look for negative intentions. This is hardly ever the case. Choices serve needs as people see them and may not always be productive; in fact, sometimes they are counterproductive. To advocate an idea, a person raises his voice. While there is nothing wrong with the intention, the loud voice is counterproductive. The word *available* in this principle implies that choices outside a person's or group's perspective may represent additional options. The person who raises his voice, for instance, may not know that pausing before speaking would have the effect of underscoring the importance of the statement. Had he known, he likely would have selected a pause before speaking rather than a louder voice to make his point.

"What could the possible benefit of that be?" is a useful question for group members to ask when confronted with puzzling behavior. Assign the most generous interpretation to the person's or group's actions. This principle serves facilitators as well as group members as it helps them remain nonjudgmental. Judging closes the choices one has for perceiving and behaving. Research in dynamic teams finds that groups with more positivity than negativity are significantly more effective. More on this finding is presented in Chapter 5.

5. Facilitation takes practice. Several authors, Malcolm Gladwell (2008) among them, have been pointing out that in any field, expertise is not a matter of talent but of practice. As they were awarded Kennedy Center Honors in 2010, Merle Haggard and Paul McCartney both were described as geniuses. A misnomer, Matthew Syed (2010) would say. While talent was certainly a factor in these two men's careers, the overriding source of their expertise was intense interest and almost daily practice beginning in their teen years. Tennis champs Venus and Serena Williams began learning to play tennis at ages 4 1/2 years and 3 years old respectively. Later in their development, their father would fill a shopping cart with 550 balls and feed them across the net to the girls one at a time. When they were finished, he would pick up the balls and start again. Charise Pempengo was in singing contests at age 7 to support her family. Olympic short track speed skating gold medalist Apolo Anton Ohno did his first skating at age 6. He says about his all-out effort at everything he attempts, "If I have given my all and still do not win, I haven't lost. Others might remember winning or losing; I remember the journey." Michael Jordan was cut from his high school basketball team. "What will you do?" asked his mother. Michael said, "I will practice."

Expertise in any field, as noted above, takes learning and practice. Since teacher leaders, and even principals and staff developers, have limited time to practice collaborative work or facilitation, none can approach the 10,000 hours that Gladwell suggests (2008). Educator facilitators can rely on three aspects to develop their facilitation chops. One area is teaching, for many of the patterns in teaching are similar to what one does when working with groups. Secondly, they can study the craft by reading books such as this, attending workshops, or observing colleagues. Reflection is a third resource. This includes careful planning and reflection after the fact. What went well? What surprises were there? What might have been done differently? The deep learning of immediate reflection invites us to pause and reinvent ourselves as practitioners. The four chapters of Section IV address developing facilitation skills.

6. Wait not for trust; practice trusting behaviors. Trust is essential to improving schools (Forsyth, Adams, & Hoy, 2011). Several dispositions working in concert lead to trust. These include integrity, concern, competence, and reliability (Kruse & Louis, 2009). Trust among teachers is linked to higher student achievement (Tschannen-Moran, 2004), and principal behavior sets a foundation for creating trusting relationships (Bryk & Schneider, 2004). Hargreaves and Shirley (2011) report community organizing to be related to higher levels of teacher-parent trust, a stronger sense of school community, a more achievement-oriented culture, and a greater degree of parent involvement in school when compared with schools with less involvement. Groups sometimes believe they can't do important work until trust is present. Yet waiting for trust is like waiting for Godot. In the absurdist play by Samuel Beckett, two characters, Vladimir and Estragon, wait endlessly and in vain for someone named Godot, who never appears. One doesn't wait for trust; one identifies trusting behaviors and begins to practice them. Problems like trust and communication can never be solved, but identifying and practicing the behaviors of each will lead to effective working conditions. Thus, groups develop by using inclusion activities that provide needed opportunities for trust building. Starting each meeting by answering for oneself the question "Who am I in relationship to this group?" becomes crucial to bringing everyone into the physical and emotional space. Mylene Keipp, a colleague of mine in the Los Angeles Unified School District, shared with me that at a meeting at which multiple districts were represented, a principal asked her, "How is it that your group seems to gel, even with different ages, backgrounds, perspectives, etc?" She replied, "We start every meeting with group development. Last week, we learned about our first jobs. Today we shared a partial bucket list."

Awestruck, the principal responded, "Every meeting?" With a beaming smile, Mylene said, "Yes. That's how we learn more about who we are as a team." Although her group had clashing personalities, they overcame their personal idiosyncrasies to meet the collective needs of their schools and district. These skills are probed in Section III.

7. Simple and less are better than complicated and more. Groups develop with facilitators' help. Groups and facilitators first master a few sound strategies and use them frequently until they are comfortable with them. A description of 150 strategies can be found in Appendix A of *The Adaptive School: A Sourcebook for Developing Collaborative Groups* (2009). An administrator in Lincoln, Nebraska, used the same strategy, the Focusing Four, 17 times with 17 different groups to generate data for a strategic plan. She could have varied her strategy, but finding one that worked, she repeated it. Expect that some groups may transform into owners of their learning and ask self-directed questions such as, "We are pretty comfortable with First Turn/Last Turn. Could we try Text Rendering today?"

8. Attend to energy. Margaret Wheatley observes that the quality of human relationships is the energy source for work in organizations (2006). Daniel Pink (2011) observes that humans don't become engaged by being controlled, threatened, or motivated by external sources, but that these motivations are within each of us and are the sources of our actions and values. Physics has explained invisible energy sources with which humans interact. Some of the more obvious are gravitational pull, electrostatic fields, inertia, and centrifugal forces. While they cannot be observed directly, they are known through their effects. The ball falls from our hand; we label gravity as a cause. Five such human fields, or states of mind, are *efficacy, flexibility, craftsmanship, consciousness,* and *interdependence* (Costa & Garmston, 2002). High-performing groups find ways to maintain their energy in order to reach high-level goals. The process of continuous self-improvement requires forces that fuel learning and action. These five forces are needed to power through obstacles and effectively resolve conflicts. Group members are only able to absorb new learning and meet new challenges by maintaining high levels of collaborative energy. We see the effects of the levels of energy in group members' attitudes, language, and actions.

WAYS TO USE THIS BOOK

This book has been designed with flexibility in mind. Your own learning style and interests should determine how best you use it. If you have picked it up because of a general interest in working with groups, you may wish to start at the beginning and read it all the way through. If you are seeking inspiration and validation that collaboration is the right work and it is working in real schools, you may want to begin your reading with Chapter 1, Building Effective Groups, and Chapter 5, Forming Smarter Groups. If you are trying to solve a particular dilemma or to figure out how to improve an aspect of facilitation or group development, the table of contents may guide you to sections of most value. If you are using it as text in a course to inform school leaders, teacher leaders, and others about ways to get the most out of groups, you may wish to develop a course outline based on this content.

Section I explains the nuts and bolts of getting the work done. At successful meetings, a maximum amount of work is completed in minimum time with a maximum amount of member satisfaction. The work requires a clear understanding of group members' roles, the group's and others' decision-making authority, and what constitutes an effective agenda. This section gets specific about the tasks involved in group work and offers some simple strategies for improving how the group accomplishes these goals.

Section II explores the concept of collective intelligence in groups and the factors that bring about a group that is greater than the sum of its parts. Group members must understand that the way individuals talk with one another matters greatly to the group's effectiveness. Groups whose members are careful to distinguish between discussion and dialogue will find it easier to seek solutions and make decisions. Group members who are willing to reflect and assess their own thinking will be able to surface hidden assumptions that can hinder their own growth and that of the group, and will be able to help colleagues move forward. Understanding members' mental models and hidden assumptions enhances the group's ability to approach work in ways that are more likely to result in success. Finally, effective groups understand the value and benefits in constructive rather than destructive conflict.

In Section III, I discuss the understandings that characterize the work of groups that are working for or moving into a more mature stage. Becoming a self-directed group requires self-managing, self-monitoring, and self-modifying. Effective groups are able to develop the five sources of energy to sustain their work and keep them moving forward. Mature groups also have a deep sense of collective efficacy.

Finally, in Section IV, I present some ideas for teacher leaders and others who wish to develop skills as citizen facilitators. Facilitation is a learned skill that takes practice. Attention to particular aspects of facilitation, choosing language to use, knowing when to intervene, and setting the stage for maximum impact all lead to a greater comfort level and improved productivity.

SECTION I

Getting Work Done

1

Building
Effective Groups

Meetings are becoming teachers' work. Evidence increasingly shows that collaborative cultures lead to higher student achievement (Hoy, Tarter, & Hoy, 2006; Louis, Marks, & Kruse, 1996). Effective and time-efficient meetings have obvious benefits. Well-organized meetings result in groups that produce work important to students; in addition, they promote members' satisfaction and capacity to collaborate, and therefore their willingness to conscientiously contribute. The more groups succeed in getting important work done in meetings, the greater their sense of collective efficacy, a resource undeniably linked to student success (Hoy et al., 2006). Finally, members of successful groups ultimately become members and leaders elsewhere in the system and enrich the quality of work within the school and district.

It is in meetings that teachers work together to improve instructional practice and performance. It is in meetings that teachers clarify policies, identify and address problems, assess standards, and modify schedules. It is in meetings that faculties respond to the changing needs of students, standards, and curriculum demands. It is in meetings that groups mature and manage differences. And it is in meetings that their working culture evolves—or stays the same.

Professional cultures are emerging in schools, and meetings are serving a central role in improving student learning. Sustaining these collaborative, results-focused working relationships requires leaders at all levels of the organization to develop new ways of seeing their work and new templates and tools for engaging collective energy toward common goals. Not only are collaborative groups more effective at complex tasks than individuals working alone, but the group's collective intelligence can be developed.

Most of what we know about meetings in which people plan, solve problems, and make decisions can be attributed to Michael Doyle and David Strauss. In 1976, they published a book called *How to Make Meetings Work*. This codified the best practices for meeting preparation, defining an agenda, facilitating a meeting, managing recording, dealing with disruptions, and other aspects of organizing successful meetings. Their work originated from a project in which they recorded meetings, searching for the fewest common elements that had the greatest impact on successful outcomes. They examined meetings of the boards of directors of institutions such as banks and of less complex organizations like PTAs.

Their work identified five standards that I have seen, time and time again, improve group effectiveness. I often tell groups that these standards will guarantee success, as measured by maximum amount of work done in minimum time with maximum member satisfaction. Actually, on some occasions I have taught the standards and then returned months later to observe progress, only to find no progress at all. The point is that the standards alone are not sufficient; it is how groups work with the standards that makes a difference. Beyond merely introducing the standards, how a group maintains them while moving through the inevitable implementation dip that accompanies any innovation will predict the group's success in that measure—maximum work done, minimum time, maximum member satisfaction.

FIVE STANDARDS FOR EFFECTIVE MEETINGS

The implementation of these five standards leads to meeting success:

- Address only one topic at a time.
- Use one process at a time.
- Balance participation and make meetings interactive.
- Use cognitive conflict productively.
- Have everyone understand and agree to meeting roles.

Address Only One Topic at a Time

Most of us have experienced the confusion that occurs when a group gets off track. For example, teachers are deliberating over which textbooks to select, and someone mentions that some books are housed in the supply room, leading to a discussion of the orderliness of the supply room and then why no one has cleaned it up yet. This discussion will drive the linear-minded among us nuts, take the meeting in a different direction, and create confusion and frustration.

Who is responsible for keeping the group on track—a facilitator or group members? The answer is both. While a facilitator remains neutral on content, he or she is in charge of process and monitors and redirects the group when necessary. However, informed group members can and should gently remind peers of their agreement to work in accordance with the five standards of effective meetings.

A facilitator might ask, in a spirit of inquiry, "Help us understand how that relates to our topic." More often than not, the group member will note that the item can be saved for another part of the meeting. Sometimes we are surprised when the participant explains how the idea does, in fact, relate. Another facilitator move is to record the new idea on a flip chart, commenting, "This is important; let's record it here so we don't lose it." Groups appreciate having these comments recorded for later because it keeps the conversation on track yet respects participants and semirelated ideas.

The role of group members, or what Bruce Wellman and I call "engaged participants" (2009), is significant. They frequently guide and help the group stay on track with questions, such as: "I'm confused. Are we still discussing . . ."; "Could you help us understand how your comment connects to this topic?"; or "That's a good thought. Can we save it for later when we get to topic X?" Pointing out where in the conversation the speaker's point may be more relevant can help the speaker feel recognized, but gently guide the conversation back to the issue at hand.

Use Only One Process at a Time

By *process*, I mean any strategy used to deliberate about content. Doyle and Strauss (1976) make a useful distinction between *process* and *content*, describing the former as "chewing" and the latter as "gum." "Chewing" anything, including information, is essential when the goal is understanding.

Brainstorming is an example of a process the rules of which are often violated. The ground rules for brainstorming are to accept and list all contributions without criticism or questions. The moment a question is asked about an item, the process breaks down and a rambling conversation is likely to ensue rather than a return to brainstorming. The facilitator should at once intervene. "Stop," she should say. "Please save that question for later." When each participant knows what process will happen following brainstorming, the group will find it easier to exercise self-discipline to stick to the protocol.

To be certain each member understands the protocol to be used, a facilitator can use a PAG/PAU strategy. In the PAG (process as given) phase, the facilitator outlines the process and the rules for what group members should and shouldn't do. Then the facilitator checks group members' understanding during the PAU (process as understood) phase. The facilitator might ask, "So, what are the ground rules?" "How much time will this take?" "What will you do if you have a question?"

Implicitly, the group has now given the facilitator permission to intervene when an agreed-on process is not followed.

Make Meetings Interactive

Even dedicated, determined group members will be unable to keep information stored in short-term memory without having time to interact with the material. Sitting and listening for lengthy periods is an ineffective way to have human beings retain ideas. The most heroic efforts of group members to stay alert will fail if members are not allowed to engage and be thoughtfully productive, such as in a Pair-Share in which a participant turns to a neighbor and synthesizes what is being said. Any meeting that runs beyond 20 to 30 minutes without group members being directed to check their perception and cement their learning is probably burning out brain cells. Groups can learn a variety of strategies for interaction. In one, members turn to one another and summarize the most important point of the preceding discussion. In another strategy, pairs identify concerns about a topic before a general discussion begins. In yet another, subgroups read and discuss a policy statement to identify concerns to suggest to the full group for discussion. See Garmston and Wellman (2009) for 150 interactive strategies.

Use Cognitive Conflict Productively

When group members bring different points of view and opinions to a discussion, the discussion will lead to better decisions, greater commitment to the outcome, and more follow-through on the decision than in groups that lack such cognitive conflict (Amason, Thompson, Hochwater, & Harrison, 1995). Using the tools described in Chapter 6, groups can learn to set aside *affective conflict*, in which members direct their anger at individuals rather than ideas, and can learn to respect individuals even while disagreeing with their points of view.

Cognitive conflict is essential to high-performing groups. This may seem counterintuitive. Many boards I have dealt with believe that disagreement is a sign of dysfunction. This could not be further from the truth. Cognitive conflict, when members disagree gracefully, is essential to improved outcomes and decision making. Effective groups use norms and tools that allow members to express their differences, to examine assumptions and mental models underlying their different points of view, and to use resolution techniques that provide for the best possible decision. The *best possible* decision may not be each member's first choice, but the pooling of thought and best understanding from all members allows better thinking to arise.

In contrast, ineffective groups either avoid conflict and have members who don't speak out for fear of not "going with the flow," or personalize conflict and blame an individual for having a contrary opinion. Avoiding cognitive conflict leads to poor decisions often made by the leader or the most vocal member of the group. Personalizing cognitive disagreement creates a host of negatives including apathy, balkanization, decreased commitment to the group's purposes, and, always, poor decisions. David W. Johnson and Roger T. Johnson have researched and written extensively about using conflict constructively. (See their website at http://www.co-operation.org.)

One volunteer board I'm familiar with had regular disagreements over matters large and small, but still was able to come to decisions that generally, when the vote was taken, were unanimous. However, a few members of the board were unhappy that the outcomes did not always completely reflect their opinions even while they ostensibly supported the group decisions by voting for them. They began to criticize the group leader for "causing conflict" and attacked the group for being "broken" because discussion reflected multiple ideas. In the end, the group ousted its chair, numerous other members resigned as a result, and only those of a similar mindset were left on the board. We will see what kinds of decisions the group makes, but I am certain that the absence of any alternative views will lead to much worse decisions and bodes ill for the future of the organization.

It takes time and group maturity for groups to develop the ability to use cognitive conflict productively. The same is true for the next meeting principle, agreeing on roles. For those reasons, both principles are explored in greater depth in later chapters.

Agree on Roles

The most influential role in any group is the role of group member or active participant. Skilled members who know meeting standards and group processes are able to work in harmony across differences to get the greatest value from meeting time. Groups that engage in decision making, planning, or problem solving need a facilitator as well as someone who will take the role of recorder. (In smaller groups, the facilitator does this.) Often, one member of the group is a decision maker—a person with role authority such as the principal, or someone with knowledge-based authority, such as a subject or curriculum specialist for the topic being discussed. Using the decision maker or most knowledgeable person as facilitator robs the group of valuable knowledge that those members can contribute to the discussion. Persons in these roles do the group the most good by functioning as an engaged group member.

Effective principals, superintendents, and content experts shy away from the role of facilitator. Chapter 2 explains why and details the responsibilities of the group member, facilitator, recorder, and leader.

INTRODUCING THE STANDARDS

One way to familiarize the group with these five standards is to use part of a meeting to have members list what they like and dislike about their meetings. Usually, enough dissatisfaction emerges about meeting practices that the group is open to learning new ways of doing business.

Another approach is to provide reading material describing the five principles. A good source is the article "The 5 Principles of Effective Meetings" (Garmston, 2006). Use a variety of reading protocols to have participants read, consider, and adopt the principles. Do not, at this time, attempt to modify these principles. A great deal of research and experience serves as a foundation for their effectiveness. Some leaders insist that the principles be followed and assessed at each meeting for at least six sessions. After at least that much experience, a conversations about adaptations may be warranted.

Providing a rationale and discussion on professional communities and why collective work is important to student learning is always a good idea. The work of Karen Seashore Louis and her colleagues (1996) is a good source, as is the synthesis of research in *The Adaptive School* (Garmston & Wellman, 2009). The findings are clear: Groups that are collectively responsive to students' needs and willing to work collaboratively to refine instruction and curriculum show remarkable increases in student learning. Knowledge of how professional communities work provides a compelling rationale for staffs to look at their own practices, including how they manage meetings.

According to Rick DuFour (2004), a professional learning community proponent, an effectively functioning group exhibits three key features. The group

- ensures student learning,
- develops professional collaboration, and
- focuses on results.

So to introduce principles of effective meetings, provide information or start a conversation that either highlights shared dissatisfaction with current practices or offers a vision of how the group's meetings might be more productive and satisfying.

ASSESSING THE STANDARDS

Periodically reviewing the five meeting standards can help remind the group about effective processes and help members

Table 1.1   Five Meeting Standards

Rate how well you believe the group followed our agreed meeting standards. Mark an X under the rating for each standard, with 1 being low and 5 being high.

	1	2	3	4	5
Addressed one topic at a time.					
Used one process at a time.					
Balanced participation.					
Used cognitive conflict productively.					
Understood and followed meeting roles.					

Source: Garmston & Wellman, 2002

reflect about their work. Set up times and create a structure for the group to reflect. Distribute a Likert-type scale questionnaire at the end of each meeting (Garmston & Wellman, 2002, p. 139). Ask members to rate each item from 1 to 5.

The group agrees to designate one person (it may be the same person or a different group member each time) to collect the forms and tally the results. The designated individual should create a visual representation that shows the data and the distribution of responses. The chart or graph should be on display as group members enter the room at the next meeting. The first task is to review the data and respond to the question, "Based on how we assessed ourselves at the last meeting, what should we work on today?"

2

Understanding Group Roles

"Learning is no longer preparation for the job; it is the job," according to a 2010 report by the National Commission on Teaching and America's Future (NCTAF). The authors go on to say that the "era of isolated teaching, working alone to meet the myriad needs of students is neither educationally effective nor economically viable in the 21st century." In an earlier report, the Commission noted that up to 46% of teachers leave their classrooms in the first five years of teaching, citing as reasons isolation, lack of support, lack of influence, and inadequate time to collaborate (NCTAF, 2003).

In schools in which collaboration is the norm, teachers are engaged in types of constructivist learning similar to that which they lead in classrooms. In grade-level and department teams, in horizontal and cross-discipline teams, and in formal professional learning communities, teachers plan, execute, reflect, learn from studying the effects of their work on student progress, and continue this cycle toward deeper understanding and richer student accomplishment. They are aided in this work by protocols that permit inquiry and productive conflict with an absence of affective or emotional conflict.

Collaboration is at the heart of getting work done in schools. "It is increasingly common for individuals to work in collaborative groups rather than alone. One finds this trend in a growing number of domains, from business and management to government and media to science and academia" (Verdoux, 2011).

Collaboration occurs within disciplines as well as across disciplines, grade levels, departments, and faculties. It occurs in pairs, trios, and large groups. It occurs spontaneously and when planned. It happens in meetings. I regard collaboration as what takes place when teams of individuals of unequal resources work together as equals to complete work. Resources always vary. Group members have different experiences, cognitive styles, educational beliefs, roles, and knowledge about the topic. Working as equals means that all contribute without reservation the very best they can toward the group's efforts.

Of the roles typically associated with meetings in which the goal is collaboration, the group member's role is most crucial to meeting success. According to some in the education field, we've been training the wrong people about effective meetings. When we train facilitators, we instill knowledge and skills into a small minority of a group's composition. When we train group members, we affect the very fiber and ethos of a group.

Make no mistake about it, the complex work that teams perform requires a facilitator who can keep an eye on process while the important content work goes on. But facilitating for a small team requires adjustments to the interactive model of meetings in which a facilitator must be neutral to content. Thus emerges a role I am going to call the *citizen facilitator*.

The five roles most commonly associated with collaborative, school-based meetings, then, are the engaged participant, the facilitator, the recorder, the person with role or knowledge authority, and the citizen facilitator.

What Is Effective Collaboration?

Pat Wilson O'Leary, a Michigan consultant, told me with a twinkle in her eye that when she first learned about cooperative learning, she would put her students in groups and tell them to cooperate. *C-o-o-p-e-r-a-t-e*, she would have them spell. Collaboration, like cooperative learning, is far more complex than that, and we do educators a disservice when we assume that we all are naturally equipped to do it.

One fundamental principle of effective collaboration is that members share the intention to make meetings worth their time. Regardless of the group member's formal role, each member contributes to ensuring that meetings work and that they lead to a worthy outcome. In short, any group is always the group's group. In any session in which exploring, planning, reflecting, or problem solving occur, the engaged participants—or group members—do the work of the meeting.

Most importantly, the purpose of collaborating is to achieve collective results that participants would not be able to accomplish working alone. Expected outcomes include shared objectives, a sense of urgency and commitment, a sense of belonging, open communication, mutual trust and respect, realizing complementary diverse skills and knowledge, intellectual agility, interdependence in framing goals and approaches, and individual latitude in carrying out a design the group arrived at jointly.

The characteristics of ideal teacher collaboration are these:

- It is voluntary.
- Teachers believe that each individual's contribution is valued equally.
- It requires a shared goal.
- Leadership is distributed.

If teachers are working on poorly defined goals, they may unintentionally be working on different goals.

Collaboration involves shared responsibility for decisions and outcomes. It is based on shared resources that might include time, expertise, skills in group dynamics, or other assets. While some degree of trust and respect among participants is needed at the outset of collaborative activities, trust and respect do not have to be central characteristics of a new collaborative relationship. As teachers become more experienced in collaborating, their relationships will be characterized by the trust and respect that grow within successful working groups.

The levels of complexity, interdependence, skills, maturity, and leadership required to attain high levels of collaboration are staggering. Arriving at real collaboration does not happen simply by forming a group, especially when school cultures traditionally have valued and supported independence over interdependence.

MEETING ROLES

The typical roles in a group are the engaged participant, the facilitator, the recorder, and the role authority. I am adding a special role, that of citizen facilitator. Groups should be familiar with these roles.

The participant is most critical to the meeting and school success, provided that the participant actively engages in the group. Group members become active participants by developing habits that foster the group's intentions, by consciously acting to further the group's purpose, and by taking an active role in the group's work.

Many learning teams rotate the roles of facilitator and recorder to allow those acting in the roles to engage more as a group member, or may decide in very small groups that the facilitator is what I am calling a citizen facilitator, who actively participates in the meeting while facilitating at the same time.

Schools must provide training for teachers to effectively assume collaborative roles and learn facilitation skills. To require collaboration without helping individuals develop the skills to do so is tantamount to malpractice. See Chapter 11 on developing facilitation skills.

The Engaged Participant

Every person in the meeting who is not facilitating, recording, acting as "the boss," or acting as a guest has the most important role in the room—that of engaged participant. Engaged participants—group members—do the actual work of the meeting. In fact, the meeting's success depends more on informed participation from the group members than on any individual's skills and knowledge, including those of a group member with role authority, or a content expert, or a facilitator.

Anyone, at some time, might be an engaged participant. Members of standing committees, participating guests at a special session, the recorder or facilitator before or after serving in those roles, and the building administrator can all at some time serve as engaged participants. What these group members know and do is critically important to group effectiveness.

In strong groups, engaged participants monitor their personal adherence to the meeting standards described in Chapter 1. They notice and set aside comments they are about to make if the comment would violate the "one topic at a time" standard, for example. They also monitor the group's adherence to standards. Engaged participants perform these important functions in meetings:

Gatekeeping. Ochan might say to Antoine, "Antoine, I'm aware that you haven't said anything for a little while. Is there anything that you would like to add?" Another person makes a comment, "Allyce, from where I'm sitting, your eyebrows look furrowed. Any comments you'd like to add?"

Setting and testing working agreements. It's appropriate for a group member to initiate a conversation that sets a working agreement, such as starting meetings on time. Later, if the agreement is not being met, a group member might test the agreement by commenting that the agreement is not being met and asking what needs to happen for the group to keep to its agreement.

Testing consensus. It is not necessary to wait for the facilitator to test for consensus. A member might ask for a show of hands to see if the group has reached consensus on a topic.

Monitoring internal processes. Engaged participants become aware of when they have stopped listening to others and are following a train of thought in their own minds. They recognize their emotional responses to other speakers. When they are irritated, they notice it, but instead of giving in to the irritation, they locate the probable reason. Then they set the feeling aside so they can stay fully engaged in the conversation.

The Facilitator

To facilitate means "to make easier." The facilitator directs the procedures that the group will use in the meeting, choreographs the group's energy to shift activities as necessary to maintain momentum, and helps keep the group focused on meeting standards, including one content and one process at a time (Garmston & Wellman, 2009). The facilitator may stand while group members remain seated, clearly delineating the separation between the two and indicating the difference in roles. Most importantly, professional facilitators maintain obvious content neutrality in the group's discussions, dialogue, and actions.

Facilitators guide groups in planning, solving problems, and reflecting with planned agendas and selected protocols. Yet the unexpected can and frequently does happen. Facilitation, like teaching, is cognitively complex and has the added tensions associated with performing leadership functions in front of colleagues. While the facilitator learns to be content neutral, a provision exists for getting the facilitator's voice into the room when someone in this role feels a strong need to be heard. Called Signal Role Change, this strategy requires the facilitator to move to a different part of the room and use a different tone to offer the group an idea. Better yet, the facilitator asks a member to facilitate the meeting for a while to allow her to participate. The old adage that actions speak louder than words is true, and if the facilitator does not make one of these moves, some in the group will be confused and wonder if the facilitator is trying to manipulate the meeting outcome.

Facilitation is information intensive, and new research casts shadows on George Miller's 1956 research that found that a person could hold seven items in working memory (plus or minus two) depending on levels of stress and external conditions (Miller, 1963). According to Nelson Corwin at the University of Missouri-Columbia, the human brain can actually hold about four items at a time, and even then it depends on the complexity of the items (Rock, 2009).

Then how do accomplished facilitators attend to the group's progress on the agenda, to what more the group needs to do to reach its goal, and to what is being recorded? How do they monitor members' moods, energy levels, and cognitive contributions, and how do they select from their repertoire of facilitation strategies to respond appropriately to the moment? We find that they do not think dozens of moves ahead but, like the rest of us, only a few. Through experience and study, facilitators at the top of their game have learned to chunk information in such a way that each move they envision can activate a series of maps in the prefrontal cortex. These maps are informed through experience and by embedding routine patterns into states of automaticity.

Kendall Zoller (2010) suggests that facilitators memorize the first 5 minutes of any planned interaction with a group. So saying hello, establishing rapport, getting group members' permission to facilitate the meeting, and framing the agenda all are held as routines within the chunk Start the Meeting.

Facilitators learn to facilitate by practicing patterns until the patterns become embedded as chunks they can call upon as needed, in much the same way that classical ballet dancers learn complex routines. Rather than memorize a routine step by step, some long sequences are part of classical patterns that the dancers routinely follow. For each of the following relatively routine procedures in managing a meeting, experienced facilitators have embedded routines that allow them to perform these tasks without burdening the prefrontal cortex, which involves what we sometimes term the conscious brain.

- Call the meeting to order.
- Establish norms.
- Frame the goal.
- Check for understanding.
- Keep only one process happening at a time.
- Maintain focus on only one topic at a time.

- Elicit language specificity.
- Mediate conflicts.
- Test for consensus.
- Intervene when events may sidetrack the group.
- Close the meeting appropriately.

Decisions related to these functions are routine for experienced facilitators. One problem, of course, in developing teacher leaders or other school-based educators as facilitators is that making these functions routine requires hours of practice.

In sum, the facilitator

- remains neutral on content,
- clarifies his or her role with the group,
- focuses group energy,
- keeps the group on task,
- directs processes,
- encourages everyone to participate,
- protects participants and ideas from attack,
- contributes to agenda planning, and
- elicits clarity regarding meeting follow-up.

The Recorder

At the best of times, human minds can manage only limited amounts of information in their working memories. At the end of a long day, when people are tired, or when people are under stress, short-term memory suffers.

Group members who are cognitively engaged in the flow of a conversation or in processing ideas may find that their ability to retain auditory information fades. In addition, the brain can hold only one visual representation of an object at a time (Rock, 2009). Publicly charting and posting the group's data is a critical process for helping members' working memories.

Like most facilitators, recorders should be purposefully neutral. They support the group by focusing on the task—maintaining a clear visual representation of important ideas and data and supporting the facilitator in managing group processes as effectively and efficiently as possible.

The recorder may also help the facilitator or the group set up the visual records, arrange the room, or manage other physical aspects of the meeting as needed.

In sum, the recorder

- remains neutral to content,
- supports the facilitator,
- records basic ideas as the facilitator paraphrases them,
- keeps eyes on charts and not on group members,
- writes legibly using uppercase and lowercase printing,
- uses alternating colors to separate ideas,
- uses icons and simple graphics, and
- keeps all charts visible to support group memory.

The Role Authority

As meetings more and more become teachers' work, school leaders learn to pass on some of the hats they have traditionally worn, such as facilitator. In some group work, the principal's knowledge, values, and experience are more useful as a member of the group than as a leader. The principal or other authority (assistant principal, content expert, or department chair) is a resource to the group as it makes decisions.

Before and after the meeting, the role authority

- coordinates the agenda design,
- develops group member leadership,
- coordinates the activities of subcommittees,
- sees that meeting follow-through occurs, and
- provides for evaluation of the meeting.

During the meeting, the role authority

- informs the group of any constraints and resources,
- advocates for his or her own ideas,

- inquires about others' ideas, and
- actively participates.

Principals may need to examine their own issues of power and control: What does being in charge mean when you are not running the meeting? Leaders can address the challenge of sharing leadership by seeking advice from other principals and letting go of the reins in stages. They can try to refocus on their ideas and information, rather than the role of leading the meeting. In most meetings for district leaders I have attended, the superintendent rarely runs the meeting but leaves that role to someone else so as to be fully focused on the meeting content.

In one case, I knew a principal who frequently interjected comments in faculty meetings, taking up most of the air space. When I asked her what her goals were for the group, she told me she wanted teachers to become interdependent. When she became aware of how her behavior was thwarting that goal, she monitored and adjusted her choices.

The Citizen Facilitator

In smaller groups (around three to six participants), the classic role of the facilitator simply may not work. The admonition to be content neutral, for example, or to remain standing throughout the meeting to maintain role clarity, may not be practical when the person facilitating also needs a voice in the conversation. It is important, then, to distinguish between a "professional" facilitator—one who facilitates larger groups, or groups in which the facilitator's voice is not required—and "citizen" facilitators, who have a role in situations in which the group's thinking would be incomplete without the facilitator's voice.

In small groups, the facilitator's ideas may need to be heard and the facilitator may be part of the whole. In groups such as learning teams, the role of facilitator may more appropriately be assigned to an active member of the group, and group members may find a more active participatory role by taking the role of citizen facilitator.

A citizen facilitator may be designated for the life of the group or for a semester or longer. The citizen facilitator acts as

- a two-way conduit for communications between the team and the principal, informing the team of the principal's priorities and requests, and the principal of the group's ideas and recommendations;
- a professional developer for the group, providing foundational knowledge about group processes, distinguishing between dialogue and discussion, and offering tools for conversing, planning, and problem solving; and
- the person in the group who maintains a macro perspective, using a "balcony view" to anticipate and assess periods when members are stuck or fatigued, and who initiates processes to get energy and information flowing again.

Groups with citizen facilitators want facilitated conversations but do not have access to an outside facilitator or are small enough to work at having group members develop the knowledge and skills themselves. The designated facilitator continues to maintain an active voice within the room, but develops the necessary knowledge and skill base of a facilitator. The citizen facilitator suggests approaches to the group's work, takes on charting responsibilities, and reminds the group to get back on task.

The citizen facilitator may

- work with the group (either in the meeting or through premeeting communication) to develop the agenda;
- determine whether topics are within the group's sphere of influence and appropriate to pursue;
- clarify the meeting's purpose;
- begin the meeting;
- Clarify the five standards for successful meetings;
- intervene to change behavior that detracts from the group's work;

- describe the group's goal or outcome—what members will see or hear when the work is done;
- get members to begin the conversation;
- determine whether conversation should be a dialogue (to deepen understanding) or discussion (to make decisions), and establish which discussion tools to use;
- take part in the conversation;
- check participants' understanding of tasks and processes;
- protect processes, especially the five meeting standards described in Chapter 1;
- manage the meeting flow, watching for and initiating transitions;
- push for closure;
- press for specificity, asking who will do what by when; and
- call for a meeting assessment at the end of work sessions.

Groups whose members review the roles within the group, pay attention to role responsibilities, and clearly understand as a group who will perform which role are more likely to have effective meetings and improved outcomes. These groups will mature into the collaborative, high-functioning teams that produce results.

3

Examining Decision Making

Suzanne Riley, a friend and adaptive schools colleague, told me a story about a new elementary school principal who convened a group of parents and teachers in a technology committee to explore the school's needs and to write a grant proposal for equipment. The committee worked diligently, talked with all the staff members, spent quite a bit of time studying the latest technology, read up on what direction technology might be headed in the future, and then went through an exhaustive, intense process to write a grant proposal.

Needless to say, the group was elated when the school was notified that the proposal was accepted and the school would receive the money. The money was deposited, and the principal took the committee's equipment list to the district's technology director, who looked at it and shook his head. "These computers aren't compatible with our district software," he said, "and the other equipment here isn't part of our master plan."

The committee members were outraged. They had identified what the staff in that school wanted, had secured the funding, and had done so at the principal's behest. They felt they had wasted their time, and they were understandably frustrated with the principal.

The whole situation could have been avoided if, at the beginning of the process, it was clearer to all exactly who had ultimate authority for making decisions about equipment and technology.

Effective groups are clear about decision-making authority— who decides and what decision-making processes they will use. They know in whose turf decisions lie and are sensitive to issues in which several groups might be affected or have a say.

WHO DECIDES?

Any group must determine who makes the decision related to the issue under discussion. Does the decision-making authority belong to one or more of the individuals within the group, the group as a whole, the person who convened the group, or some persons or groups not present at this meeting? Groups can be effective and productive only when they are clear about their role—whether they are responsible for providing information to those making a decision, are to make recommendations, or have the authority to make the decision themselves. Groups that lack complete clarity on this important aspect of decision making can spend a lot of time and energy discussing a matter and feel invested in it, only to find they have no ownership— like the elementary school group in the example.

The effect of not knowing who will make the final decision and what processes will be used can create broken trust. And when members lose trust in the process, groups may become embroiled in second-guessing, may become resistant, or may experience lengthy and unproductive process arguments. This robs them of time; more importantly, it saps group energy, diminishes members' sense of efficacy, and lessens their motivation to persevere on important topics.

Ideally, a facilitator introducing a topic will be thorough in describing the constraints within which the group is to work.

If not, group members might begin any discussion that may lead the group to a decision by asking essential questions about decision-making authority and processes:

- Who is making this decision?
- What processes will we use?
- What is our role in this decision?
- Are we to inform, recommend, or decide?

The question, "Who is making this decision?" can be deceptively simple. Consider all the possible levels of authority for decision-making before determining which of these is responsible for the matter at hand (Saphier, Bigda-Peyton, & Pierson, 1989):

- An individual or group with greater authority than this group's
- A single administrator deciding unilaterally
- An administrator, taking the group's input
- An administrator and staff together through consensus
- A staff with an administrator's input
- A staff by consensus
- A staff through a vote
- A subgroup of the staff with others' input
- A subgroup of the staff unilaterally
- Individual staff members, selecting from a menu of options

Members of a highly functioning group share responsibility for the group's consciousness about decision making. One rule of thumb is to clarify at least four times during the course of a meeting who is responsible for making the decision. For example, the facilitator makes the statement when introducing the topic: *We will make our recommendation to the district's technology director, who will decide . . . .* The point is reinforced during the conversation: *As we think about how we make our recommendation . . . .* The point is made again as the group reaches a conclusion: *So, your recommendation will be . . .*, and is reinforced yet again in the minutes: *The group decided to recommend to the technology director that . . . .* Why repeat? People invest emotionally in topics that are important to them and can easily put out of their minds the fact that others will have the final determination.

Another compelling reason for overcommunicating decision-making processes is the turmoil that can result when the process is unclear. I was a principal in a district in which a school needed to be closed. The superintendent made an announcement (once) and then adopted a process in which he got input from community members, following which the administrative cabinet considered the community input and added their own. Based on this input, the superintendent recommended that the Bellwether School be closed. The board accepted his recommendation, comfortable in the understanding that community members and administrators had been involved in developing the recommendations. All hell broke loose when the school to be closed was named. The superintendent was accused of having the name of the school in his desk drawer through all the deliberations. Many felt the committee work was just a sham. Although he had used a reasonable process, the superintendent had not communicated to the community, at each and every step, what the process was.

When people are upset by the outcome, they attack the process. Make sure the process is crystal clear to your group.

WHICH TOPICS ARE OURS?

Any group's interests intersect with others' turf and decision-making authority. To be efficient, groups consider coordination, effectiveness, and politics so they may honor overlapping areas of concern. The technology committee in the opening story failed at both coordination and effectiveness. To coordinate, involve members of other departments or groups that are affected or required to help implement the decision. It is both reasonable and effective to do this. The results for the technology committee were devastating to morale. After all their well-intentioned work, they were blocked from purchasing the equipment they desired.

I witnessed a high school that involved teachers in a plan to change the school schedule. Classified personnel were inadvertently neglected in the process. The planned schedule was unworkable because it lacked important perspectives from the classified group.

A politically smart group might engage a person with special knowledge, for example the assistant superintendent in charge of curriculum, in the deliberations of a curriculum committee. The assistant superintendent will know the lay of the land, what is possible and what is not, and how to support the committee's goals. Adding a school board member to a task force that ultimately will take its recommendation to the board assures that one person on the board has a deep understanding of the recommendation and can speak in its favor. A high school math team developing a list of needs might include a district-level coordinator or at least an assistant principal.

So, an essential ingredient of group success is individual and collective vigilance concerning what lies within and outside the group's influence. At some time in every group's history, this issue becomes important, whether the group is a department, a curriculum task force, an advisory group, a grade-level team, a site council, or a faculty.

Focusing the group's energy and attention only on what lies in its purview is a more efficient use of time and maintains the group's momentum in the long run—when decisions are made well and upheld, the group feels validated and supported and is more likely to maintain its momentum on the next task.

For example, many schools must address who should be responsible for decisions about policy and practices regarding student discipline. This seems like a simple question, yet it is unquestionably related to turf. Even the briefest conversation will reveal that the group must explore several interconnected questions: Are we discussing discipline within the classroom or in the school? Discipline at what level—gum or guns? Within what parameters—state law or district policies? At what level of authority—unilaterally or in consultation with the principal or parents?

Some questions group members might ask are

- Should we be talking about this?
- What parts of this issue live on our turf?
- Who are the other stakeholders involved?
- What are the roles of other groups in making decisions about this topic?
- What limitations, if any, are we bound by?

When different groups have intersecting interests, decisions become more complex. One simple and obvious example is a committee discussing a later start time for the high school. While some secondary staff might be supportive, classified work schedules are affected, as are after-school sports and part-time work schedules for some students. Busing also enters the equation, affecting the routing for middle and elementary schools. All those involved should honor collegiality and political realities to make effective decisions in the interest of attaining the goal.

LETTING GO OF IDEAS

Discussion that leads to effective decisions requires high levels of skill from group members. The Latin root of the word decision is *decidere,* meaning "to cut off or determine." Decisions require some cutting off—some release of options. When one or more individuals want a path that may not be the group's choice, that cutting off may feel very personal. It is particularly important that group members learn to discuss issues, not people, and to avoid beginning with the negative. Rather than saying, "That just won't work," or "Yes, but . . . ," try, "Another way to look at this is . . ." or "That's a good idea. What if we also . . .?" Focusing on the individual and not the idea is never

OK. Some unacceptable statements I've heard are: "I just can't discuss this anymore. Jack is always so negative" and "Adanya doesn't understand the history involved here." Group members must keep the idea separate from the person. Too often in public discourse, we confuse the two and attack an individual rather than arguing a position.

A team of fourth-grade teachers was making a decision about what needs they had and how to spend their portion of a recently-passed technology bond. They had some parameters from the district, but the principal was allowing each grade-level team leeway to purchase specific items. One teacher wanted document cameras for each classroom. The document cameras were relatively inexpensive, she argued, and easily integrated. The teachers would not need much additional training. Her colleagues were deciding by consensus, and in doing so, carefully listened to her reasoning. They even paraphrased her rationale so she knew she had been heard. However, as a group, they decided for instructional purposes to purchase camcorders.

Consensus is one approach to decision making, but not the only form. Groups sometimes vote. A major disadvantage of voting is that it creates winners and losers. Consensus softens the impact through discourse in which all views are heard and respected before final conclusions are reached.

I've learned that there are two types of consensus: *opening consensus*, which occurs through dialogue; and *focusing consensus*, which develops through discussion. These will be explored more in Chapter 6. Briefly, opening consensus means considering perspectives and possibilities, as in dialogue. These are conversations in which group members' minds are open to other views and to challenging their own assumptions; in those conversations, the members may reach common conceptual understanding. Focusing consensus means winnowing choices by clarifying criteria and applying these criteria to the choices. Making decisions about complex issues often requires that groups dialogue first.

Consensus is not a process but a value groups may hold. Full consensus would mean that everyone agrees. Schools are not organized for this form of deliberation. Unless group members are willing to commit to the process for as long as it takes, they are not usually ready for full-consensus decision making. Given most groups' constraints of time and resources, full consensus is not practical.

Groups I work with usually are better served by sufficient focusing consensus. Sufficient focusing consensus generally means that at least 80% of the group is willing to commit and to act. It also means that the others in the group agree not to block or sabotage the decision.

Sufficient focusing consensus relies on both dialogue and discussion for its effectiveness. Any dissenting voices must be able to influence and persuade 80% of the group in order to carry the day. If only a few members support one side of an issue, others respect their views and are sure they know their objections are heard and understood.

TWELVE STEPS FOR SUCCESSFUL DECISION MAKING

Here are step-by-step suggestions for groups faced with decision-making responsibility (Saphier et al., 1989):

Plan

1. Identify and explicitly state the issue, who owns it, and the underlying goal.

2. Find out and explain how much discretion you have to take action. Ask, "Must this issue be dealt with?" State how strongly you feel about it.

3. Every issue lands in someone's lap in the beginning. If it lands in yours, be sure to choose who will make the preliminary and the final decisions.

4. At the beginning of the process, communicate clearly who will make the decision and identify any constraints that will affect the scope or content of the decision (for example, staffing, budget, or time).

5. State explicitly the values you want to maintain and why they are not negotiable, if that is the case (for example, "Whatever proposals come forward, I want to hang on to small class size and the personal student-teacher contact we get from that").

Decide

6. Identify and periodically check with people as to what the full impact or consequences of a decision will be, and communicate them to all parties involved.

7. Involve all parties whose working conditions will be affected by the decision.

8. Make clear the timeline for the decision and its implementation.

9. Decide. Then explicitly state the decision or recommendations, revising it if necessary.

Implement

10. Close the loop. Communicate the decision fully and clearly to all affected parties after the decision is made, including stating how people's input was used.

11. Plan how to monitor and support day-to-day implementation of the decision and communicate these plans to everyone involved.

12. Evaluate the decision and critique the process.

Groups use these steps with explicit discussion. The model's effectiveness is based on its being public. These guidelines will help ensure that good decisions that are made stay made.

Many processes for decision making exist (see Garmston & Wellman, 2009). The Focusing Four activity described here is generically applicable to many settings and groups. I have recently been told of its success with school boards of international schools, have witnessed it being used by faculty groups and committees, and have been told that it has been used successfully with a PTA project.

Conducting a Focusing Four Consensus Activity

The four major steps in this process are to *brainstorm, clarify, advocate,* and *canvass.* This activity requires a facilitator to lead it.

The facilitator should:

1. Clarify the task and the group's role. Is the group a decision-making body, or will the group make a recommendation or inform another body or group?

2. Review each of the four steps before starting the activity.

3. Check for members' understanding.

4. Alert participants that requests to combine items may be entertained during clarification or advocacy, but that too much combining can lead to a list without meaningful distinctions.

5. Explain that the hand count or vote at the canvass stage will not determine the decision of which options to recommend. The group will decide and be guided, not bound, by the data.

6. Begin the process.

7. Assess the process. In what ways did the process support individuals and the group? What generalizations might be made about further group work, regardless of what process is being used?

The process then is outlined in these steps:

Brainstorm

- Record brainstormed ideas on chart paper.
- Elicit ideas only.

- Discourage criticisms or questions.
- Push for 12 to 18 ideas.

Clarify

- Ask if any items should be clarified.
- The author of the idea provides clarification.
- Observe the questioner during the clarification, and stop the clarification when the questioner indicates nonverbally or verbally that he or she understands.

Advocate

- Participants may advocate for as many items as they wish as many times as they wish.
- Statements of advocacy must be phrased in the positive.
- Statements of advocacy must be brief.

Canvass

- Ask individuals in the group to identify which few ideas they feel are most important.
- To define "a few," use the formula: one third plus one. (If there are 12 items on the list, ask the group to identify 5 that are most important to them. If there are 15 items on the list, ask the group to identify 6 of them.)
- Items do not have to be placed in rank order.
- Take a hand count to determine which items are of greatest interest to the group.
- Conclude by determining a process to narrow the choices down to one or two if necessary. (For an example, see Close the Discussion in Garmston & Wellman, 2009, p. 200.)

Tips

- Each step in the process must be kept separate.
- Statements of advocacy must be stated in the positive, such as "I advocate this because . . . ," and never "I don't like this because . . . ."
- Tell group members they will be guided, but not bound, by the numbers. For example, in a group of 15 members,

item A gets 9 votes and item B gets 11 votes. Such a close tally might not be a sufficient enough difference to select item B. In cases like this, the facilitator will ask the group how it wants to handle the situation.

- A rule of thumb is that if any one person objects to items being combined, the items will not be joined. The facilitator should ask anyone who sees the two items as sufficiently different that they should not be combined to raise his or her hand. This rule avoids lengthy process arguments that, in the end, do not make a difference.

- In a facilitator/recorder team, only one person directs group focus and energy. The recorder's eyes should not be on the group, but rather on the charts or facilitator.

For a DVD of the Focusing Four in action, see www.adaptive schools.com (Garmston & Dolcemascolo, 2009).

4

Creating Focused Agendas

The group was fairly large for a working team, 13 people when everyone was present. Increasingly, however, not everyone came, even though the group met only once a month. The facilitator regularly sent an e-mail a week before the meeting asking members for their input on the agenda items. The same one or two people responded almost every time. Thus, the agenda regularly reflected their ideas, along with the items left from the group's work the previous meeting.

As the facilitator created the agenda, he tried to put routine items first and deeper work later. He placed information-sharing pieces at the end of each agenda, with the result that they frequently were not heard by members who left early.

The meetings regularly resulted in little being accomplished. They were dominated by the few people who had their own unstated agendas and who used the items they placed on the group agenda to raise these issues. Lengthy discussions occurred regularly about minutiae, there were few decisions made, and little work moved forward. Many in the group remained silently resentful, and a few became openly critical; their frustration soon was directed toward others in the group. The result was a group that was largely dysfunctional.

While some issues here might be resolved with skillful facilitation and better group adherence to norms, in large part the group could be helped to function more smoothly by paying careful attention to a simple tool of effective collaboration—the agenda.

BECOMING RESULTS-ORIENTED

Creating a culture of inquiry rather than continuing to work in a culture of isolation represents a significant change within some schools. Current wisdom holds that to impact student learning, staff groups must "engage in structured, sustained, and supported instructional discussions that investigate the relationships between instructional practices and student work" (Supovitz & Christman, 2003).

Agendas become a significant tool in useful instructional conversations. Like good lesson plans, they require thought, deliberation, and careful planning. The best agendas provide an instructional focus as well as structures and protocols for collegial conversations.

Often, when educators are attempting to create cultures of inquiry, they focus initially on planning special events, arranging schedules, and other administrivia. At first it is tough to get departments, grade-level teams, articulation groups, student study groups, and other teams to adopt efficient processes that direct their time together toward improving student learning. Focusing instructional conversations is a major accomplishment in any meeting. Having the skills to construct an agenda based on learning outcomes and processes is essential. The right agenda template saves time, develops teams, and increases productivity. Deb Welsh, then deputy superintendent at the International School Bangkok, developed the template in Figure 4.1 for this work. Others can be found in *The Adaptive School: A Sourcebook for Developing Collaborative Groups* (Garmston & Wellman, 2009).

Figure 4.1   Agenda Template

MEETING AGENDA

Meeting outcome: Revise and finalize the rubric for the common assessment

Name of team/group: _____

Facilitator: _____   **Recorder:** _____

Other participants: _____

Starting/ending times: _____

Purposes: Understanding, Informing, Recommending, Deciding

TOPIC	PURPOSE	GUIDING QUESTIONS	BACKGROUND/ PROCESSES	PERSON/TIME
Welcome and overview of meeting outcomes and topics	Informing	What do we hope to accomplish at this meeting?	Ann will review what has been done since the last meeting and explain the outcomes and topics for this meeting.	Ann 3 min.
Inclusion activity to get voices in the room and to celebrate learning	Understanding	What learning can we celebrate this week?	We'll go round-robin to share a learning success with a student or an activity/strategy that worked.	Ann 7 min.

| Rubric for the common assessment | Deciding | ■ Does the rubric help students focus on the critical benchmarks for the unit? Are the rubric's criteria the right criteria?

■ Does the rubric adequately discriminate among degrees of understanding and proficiency? | We tried the writing rubric for the first time for the common assessment. At this meeting we will

■ Look once again at the unit's benchmarks and determine whether the criteria are the right criteria

■ Share observations about using the rubric to determine levels of understanding and proficiency. In order to do this, please bring student papers that you scored at standard, as well as above and below, and any observations you made while scoring

■ Make adjustments to the rubric based upon our observations | Sandy
60 min. |

INEFFECTIVE AGENDAS

One district, concerned about the lack of progress among its learning teams and complaints from many teachers about time-wasting meetings, collected and analyzed agendas from faculty meetings, school leadership teams, department meetings, and grade-level groups. When leaders analyzed the agendas, they found that as much as 80% of the meetings were administrivia—work that could be handled through memos or written communication. Administrivia includes things like scheduling, announcements, event organization, and compliance issues.

What people talk about matters. When meeting agendas reflect administrivia, the culture will follow. People's perceptions of what matters will become the items on the agenda.

At the International School Bangkok, administrators began working to develop a student-focused culture by analyzing 16 hours of meeting agendas to determine how much time was spent discussing teaching and learning. Department heads, instructional team leaders, and grade-level leaders all provided agendas from their meetings. More than 60% of the groups' time was spent on calendars, short-term scheduling, and discussing policies. The school's administrators and teacher leaders knew they had a problem to solve if they wanted to create a learning community in which teachers engaged in instructional conversations.

The first step was to refocus staff members' energy during the time they spent together. The most efficient and effective means of doing so was to begin with the end in mind—spend time addressing expected outcomes by stating the purpose of group time through a clearly outlined agenda.

Modeling their learning, the superintendent, administrators, and teachers facilitated staff and team meetings that were more efficient, inclusive, and focused on topics directly related to student learning. The superintendent's cabinet meetings were held in the round to demonstrate the use of the new meeting principles. The results-oriented agendas provided open time to analyze test data, examine student work, score common assessments, discuss effective lessons, and talk with other grade-level teachers.

By improving the meeting agenda, groups clarified their outcomes and purposes, reduced meeting time, and increased time spent on student learning issues. The school signaled what was important, which significantly influenced the culture.

PLANNING AND FORETHOUGHT

To plan an agenda, consider these factors.

Mindset

Building an agenda requires seeing other members' viewpoints. For example, consider the time the meeting will take place. Will it be after a full day of work, when members will be tired? Don't put a long report as the first item. Use energizing activities, such as starters that focus mental energy inside the room and on meeting tasks. What does the group already know? Avoid repeating information. If a few members are out of the loop, consider how they might get the information they need—for example, by conferring with or getting notes from another group member. How can the room be arranged to be most physically and psychologically conducive to the meeting outcomes? Is the meeting's purpose clear to all?

Relevance

Schedule items that are relevant to the entire group earlier on the agenda. Schedule those pertinent to just a few later in the meeting so those not involved can be dismissed. Paying attention to relevance avoids frustrating those to whom the items mean less. Cluster related items. Make sure that the meeting's items are clearly related to the larger purpose and context of the group's work.

Information

Decide what information the group needs in order to do its work. Will members need history or context? Who can provide the relevant information? Does the group need policy background or supporting research? Who will seek out and provide that kind of knowledge? Will members need the information in advance? How will the group handle it if some members do not prepare ahead of the meeting—or will the group process the information together? How much time will be needed to do so? What are the next steps, and who will be involved?

Interaction

Plan degrees and types of interaction. Groups that do all their work as a whole are wasting time and brain energy. We seem to be slow learners on this point. Medina writes,

> We know that the brain continuously scans the sensory horizon, with events constantly assessed for their potential interest or importance. The more important events are then given extra attention. We also know that attention wanes after about 10 minutes.

Medina continues:

> So I ask this question in every college course I teach: Given a class of medium interest, not too boring and not too exciting, when do you start glancing at the clock, wondering when the class will be over? There is always some nervous shuffling, a few smiles, and then a lot of silence. Eventually someone blurts out: "Ten minutes, Dr. Medina."
>
>   "Why 10 minutes?" I inquire.
>
>   "That's when I start to lose attention. That's when I begin to wonder when this torment will be over." The comments are always said in frustration. A college lecture is still about 50 minutes long.

Peer-reviewed studies confirm my informal inquiry: Before the first quarter hour is over in a typical presentation, people *usually* have checked out. If keeping someone's interest in a lecture were a business, it would have an 80% failure rate. What happens at the 10-minute mark to cause such trouble? Nobody knows. The brain seems to be making choices according to some stubborn timing pattern, undoubtedly influenced by both culture and genes. (2008, p. 74)

To address this problem, I apply a 10–2 formula: about 10 minutes of content followed by about 2 minutes of processing time.

Mary Budd Rowe's research also confirms this finding. In an article called "Getting Chemistry off the Killer Course List" (1983), she describes an experiment in which some teachers taught in the usual manner, while others paused about every 10 minutes and instructed students to process the information. The latter group not only exceeded the first in the end-of-course assessment but a full year later had a much greater command of the course material. Hence the 10–2 rule.

Consider what tasks the group needs to accomplish: exploring, informing, understanding, recommending, and deciding. Scaffold the meeting using *starters*, *structures*, and *sustainers* (Lipton, Wellman, & Humbard, 2003).

Starters

Starters help people shift physically, socially, cognitively, and emotionally into the work. Conversation starters are safe avenues that allow people to talk without feeling judged, make statements without risk when they are unsure, and disclose what they do not know in a way that they can be heard without embarrassment. On the other hand, simple "feel-good" openers have no connection to the work, and people often view them as time wasters. An example of a feel-good activity would be to ask participants to name their favorite movie, while an example of a targeted starter is to ask them to use Paired Verbal Fluency (see below) to try to recall every-thing they can remember from the last meeting. This carries the double value of engaging members immediately on rel-evant material and reintroducing information from the pre-ceding meeting, without which time is often lost in meetings getting started again.

Paired Verbal Fluency is an activity in which each partner talks for one minute, then each for 45 seconds, and then each finally wraps up in 20 seconds. Neither partner is allowed to repeat what the other has said.

Structures

Groups tend to avoid topics that are difficult to talk about. Like starters, structures frame the topic and the ways it will be discussed; they differ in that they frame longer conversations than starters do. The shape of the structure will determine the cognitive processes group members must use. Structures are protocols to help shape the conversation for efficiency and psychological safety. Protocols help keep conversations on track and maximize efficiency. Brainstorming is one protocol. Another is Pair-Share. Planning ahead allows for pacing, better meeting the group's needs, thoughtful response to the group's level of psychological and emotional safety, and consideration of how the protocol will be introduced.

Matchbook Definition is a structure that allows members to organize and integrate learning from a meeting. Each indi-vidual or pair develops a brief definition—one that could fit on a matchbook—of the topic being discussed. The instruc-tions stipulate that the definitions (usually 8 to 12 words) be written on a sentence strip and posted on the wall. The activ-ity lasts 6 minutes.

Many groups use the First Turn/Last Turn strategy when topics are difficult to talk about because it provides psycho-logical safety and slows the conversation down enough so that people can understand one another. Use it for relevant text or with other materials such as data, student work products, les-son plans or rubrics.

FIRST TURN/LAST TURN

PURPOSE

Scaffold for dialogue; a structure for hard-to-talk-about topics

PROCESS

- Form groups of four to eight members.
- Members read a section of text and highlight three to four items that have particular meaning for them.
- The facilitator names a person to start sharing in each group.
- Group members take turns sharing one of their items but do not comment on it. They simply name it.
- In round-robin fashion, group members comment about the item *with no crosstalk.*
- The person who initially named the item now shares his or her thinking about the item, and therefore gets the last turn.
- Repeat the pattern around the table.

VARIATIONS

- When possible, members should read the text before coming to the meeting. Allow 3 or 4 minutes for the group to review what each member marked; this will save face for those who forgot to read.
- Reading sources can include journal articles, policy statements, mission statements, a sample of student work, or original writing by members on a common topic.

(Continued)

(Continued)
FACILITATOR TIPS

- Select the first speaker geographically; for example, the person sitting with his or her back most directly against a particular wall. Using a selection method can interrupt problematic patterns in group dynamics such as having one person always be the first to speak.
- Stress that there should be no crosstalk. Explain that crosstalk takes the focus off the speaker, changes the topic, and diminishes the speaker's importance and influence.
- Relate this activity to dialogue in which the tight structure allows members to experience the emotional skills and values of dialogue. This experiential learning is important as a scaffold for learning to dialogue.
- Monitor and intervene when crosstalk begins.

Sustainers

Sustainers are verbal and nonverbal tools that help group members maintain conversations and disagree agreeably. Sustainers support group members' ability to maintain cognitively complex or emotionally risky conversations. At each moment, participants make decisions about how and when to participate. The group members' nonverbal and verbal communications give cues about safety.

Sustainers include voice, physicality, and verbal communication tools. Among the more generically useful sustainers that allow deep conversation and respectful conflict are the seven norms of collaboration. Chapter 6 describes how these habits of communication can make good teams better and mediocre teams good.

Consider the group's size and what is most effective for different types of interaction. When would the work be better handled in pairs, and when in small groups? Trios can bring different experiences, but also increase the risk of talk that is off task. Quartets bring greater diversity, but may be challenged to use new communication skills. Reflection is best done individually.

Most protocols can be adapted, with forethought, to the group's context. Particularly important is the group's maturity and how effectively members work together. The more immature the group, the greater the need for tight structures in which members have little choice about ways of participating and especially need the reasons and structures of the protocol explained. Tight protocols are also helpful for hard-to-discuss or sensitive topics.

Rationale for protocols should always be given, because knowing what, why, and how the protocol is to be used reduces group resistance and helps members engage with greater intention and effectiveness.

THE WELL-CONSTRUCTED AGENDA

How can something as simple as an agenda template have a significant impact? As can be seen in Figure 4.1, a well-designed agenda focuses on results. It shows topic, purpose, guiding questions, and background or process. A well-constructed agenda includes the following.

Meeting Outcomes

Identify the desired outcome or outcomes of the meeting. An agenda with several topics may have several outcomes. Good outcomes describe a product, not a process. Consider the intended result and what evidence would be needed to determine whether the group members should record the desired result and offer evidence that the group has achieved its desired outcomes. For example, drafting a team goal is a product. Discussing data about reading scores describes what members will do in pursuit of an outcome, but does not describe an outcome. Reviewing outcomes at the beginning of the meeting helps group members start with the end in mind.

Topics

Think about the sequence of topics. Topics launch the group into action and so should align with meeting outcomes and guiding questions. Which topic does it make sense to discuss first? What issues need to be addressed at the beginning so that the dialogue will yield information that will help the group get from the starting point to the outcome? Issues that may involve disagreements should be raised early on, so that the group can come to agreement on them before members depart. Plan an opening that sets the tone and enables participants to understand outcomes and processes. Activate prior knowledge about the first topic to get minds and voices, as well as bodies, in the room. Allow for a closing topic that ensures clarity on group decisions and next steps. Specify, on the agenda, who is to do what by when to guarantee that the meeting will end with closure.

Purpose

Label the purpose of each topic. The purpose may be

- to dialogue (explore or understand),
- to inform (announcements),
- to recommend (to another decision-making body), or
- to decide (discussion leading to a decision).

Specify the purpose of each item on the agenda as exploring, informing, understanding, recommending, or deciding. Thinking through purposes clarifies the group's role and contributes to trust as members become clear about their roles and what is expected of them in decision making. Keep information items to a minimum or eliminate them. Much information can be communicated more efficiently in other ways, such as through e-mail.

Background and Process

Construct engaging questions that encourage group members to probe topics at a deeper level before group work. Think through questions that group members need to address and in what sequence.

Summarize information that participants need before they respond to the guiding questions. What is the history that led up to the task? Define unfamiliar terms.

Describe any processes the group will use to accomplish each task. What protocols will the group use? Will group members make a decision using a consensus process? Analyze cause-and-effect relationships in the data with a fishbone diagram?

Person and Time

Identify the person responsible for each task to alert the individual to the need to prepare.

Include an estimate of the time needed for each item on the agenda. Estimating time helps ensure that the agenda has been thoughtfully constructed and the tasks are not too ambitious for the time allotted. Topics that will be addressed using a process or protocol will need extra time for explanation and modeling of that process.

If the meeting regularly runs past the time allotted, have the group consider the problem. Is the issue that conversation is being derailed by a few people? Are the times allotted for each topic unrealistic? Consider appointing a timekeeper who can remind the group when the time for an item is reached and ask the group to determine how best to make adjustments to reach its outcomes—delaying other items to continue on one topic, coming to a close on the item at hand, or deciding to continue discussion on the topic at a later time, perhaps with additional input or study by one or two members who can report back.

Perhaps most importantly, meeting planners need to apply the rule of one half. I've found this incredibly effective in supporting productive meetings. Using this rule, planners identify all the items that should be on the agenda, and then cut the list in half. Doing so trades coverage for depth and leads to better results for students and greater satisfactions for participants.

The Importance of an Agenda

If we want to improve student learning in our schools, we must improve our professional practices. Being effective and efficient with our collaborative time is essential. An agenda template can be a powerful device for advancing our work so that we can focus on our core purpose—student learning.

SECTION II

Developing Collaborative Communities

5

Forming Smarter Groups

Most of us have been part of a group that has not worked very well. Some individuals may have dominated, or not all seemed to be on the same page, or perhaps the goal for the work just wasn't clear or achievable. A few of us have been a part of a group that just clicked—and the outcome was remarkable.

What factors contribute to those groups that work? Process, surely, counts for a lot. The first section of this book is devoted to those elements that contribute to a smoother process. Other factors may be personalities of group members or good facilitation. But groups that accomplish their work seem to have an above-average ability in multiple areas—an intelligence to what they do and how they do it.

Is there such a thing as collective intelligence? If so, does it make a difference in a group's effectiveness? Is it possible to raise the IQ of working groups?

According to Anita Woolley and her colleagues, we can begin with what our mothers told us: Two heads are better than one. The whole is greater than the sum of the parts. Now it seems science is catching up to folk wisdom in discovering what the old wives' tales have long known: groups can have a collective wisdom far beyond the intelligence of individual members (Gherardi & Nicolini, 2002; Woolley et al., 2010).

From my observations working with groups around the world, I also would say that collective intelligence makes a tremendous difference in a group's ability to engage in complex cognitive work that results in improved outcomes. The group's ability to communicate, collaborate, and commiserate are common core attributes that make groups more effective. On the other hand, factors that most people would suppose make groups work better—group satisfaction, group cohesion, group motivation—actually do not, according to emerging research (Woolley et al., 2010).

In considering ways to help groups become smarter, I have three premises and want to dispel two myths. Based on new research and firsthand experience, I conclude there are specific ways to know how "smart" a group may be, predict how well the group will work, and take actions that will improve its IQ.

THREE PREMISES

Collective Intelligence Is Real

To know whether group, or collective, intelligence exists, it may be helpful to be specific about what it is. I like the definition of Thomas W. Malone, director of the MIT Center for Collective Intelligence, who said succinctly, "Collective intelligence is groups of individuals doing things collectively that seem intelligent" (2006). Anita Woolley, a researcher at Carnegie Mellon who has a Harvard doctorate in organizational behavior, has made collective intelligence a primary aspect of her research. Woolley describes collective intelligence as a "factor that explains a group's performance on a wide variety of tasks." In other words, the group's collective ability on one set of tasks can help predict its results on others, similar to findings with individual intelligence.

Woolley and colleagues conducted two studies with 699 people in which they gave subjects standard intelligence tests and then assigned them randomly to teams. They asked the teams to complete several tasks—including brainstorming, decision making, and visual puzzles—and to solve one complex problem. Then the teams were rated on how well they performed the tasks. The researchers found "substantial evidence" for the existence of collective intelligence (Woolley et al., 2010). Collective intelligence is real, and it is measurable.

Groups Are Living Things

The group has a personality of its own that is more than or different from the individuals within it. It is its own social network. Human beings are social animals. We do not operate as well independently of others. Just as some animals are herd animals— think horses or elephants—humans work best in a network. In *Connected: The Surprising Power of Our Social Networks and How They Shape Our Lives*, Nicholas Christakis and James Fowler write,

> Social networks can manifest a kind of intelligence that augments or complements individual intelligence, the way an ant colony is "intelligent" even though individual ants are not, or the way flocks of birds determine where to fly by combining the desires of each bird (2009, p. 26).

M. Mitchell Waldrop, in his book *Complexity: The Emerging Science at the Edge of Order and Chaos* (1992), expands on our knowledge of how simple patterns govern complex behaviors like the flocking of birds. Using computer simulations, researchers discovered that birds follow three simple internal instructions:

1. Maintain a minimum distance from other objects in the environment, including other birds,

2. Match the velocity of other birds in your vicinity, and

3. Move toward the perceived center of the mass of other birds in your vicinity.

We should take note that birds do not have a superintendent of birds. They internalize their "norms" of behavior just as productive groups internalize and use the seven norms of collaboration and five standards for successful meeting. In doing so, they become smarter and more resilient.

Human beings, I believe, are not always of such a like mind. That does not make the resulting group any less of its own entity. Visa cofounder Dee Hock coined the term *chaordic* to describe complex, self-organizing systems that manifest both chaotic and orderly qualities. In *The Birth of the Chaordic Age* (2000) he describes how a chaordic organization, such as the Internet, is not so much a thing as a pattern of agreements about interactions that help voluntary participants achieve certain shared goals or visions, guided by agreed-on principles. This is a foundational principle of networked individuals.

Group Intelligence Depends on Group Process

What do you hear about great groups? Not that the members are all really smart but that they listen to each other, share criticism constructively, have open minds. They're not autocratic. Groups whose members work well together produce better results, and working well is enhanced by strong commitment to a shared process. There are many approaches to team building that can help groups develop greater collaborative and collective intelligence.

TWO MYTHS

Smart People Make Smart Groups

The best teams are more than a collection of talent. Some of the worst groups are made up of the smartest people. And sometimes groups of individuals who are more average and work well together come up with brilliant ideas or solutions. It's not possible to accurately predict how well a group will perform on a task simply by averaging the IQs of its members or by having a particularly bright individual in the group. Despite what we might predict, the link between individuals' intellects and group intelligence is weak (Woolley et al., 2010).

All Groups Are Created Equal

There is no question of the power of groups. Collaboration is becoming the norm in most fields. Eric von Hippel, a professor of technological innovation in the MIT School of Management, has done case studies of how the collective body of users of a product often offer a company more innovative ideas than the company's own researchers (Von Hippel, 2005).

Brian Uzzi of Northwestern University says that more cutting-edge research across many fields is coming from teams rather than individuals, and papers with multiple authors are more often cited (Wuchty, Jones, & Uzzi, 2007a, 2007b). James Surowiecki, author of *The Wisdom of Crowds* (2005), has helped build the notion that collective thought always results in a better decision.

In an age of Wikipedia and other online collaborations brought about by the ability to connect through technology, some people become almost ecstatic about the idea of harnessing collective wisdom. Wikipedia, however, is shared knowledge. Knowledge is information, not wisdom.

Groups, particularly groups that develop their collective intelligence, are a tremendous force both for change at the individual level and in the ability to affect organizational issues. Sometimes collective decision making is good; sometimes it isn't. It works extremely well at times; sometimes it does not. The goal is to make group work effective, and have groups work at the highest level of intelligence.

THE KEY TO SMARTER GROUPS

Three individual-level features correlate to collective intelligence:

First, the greater the *social sensitivity* of group members, the smarter the group. Second, the more *turn taking* within the group, the better the group performs. And third, the more *women* in the group, the higher the group IQ.

What might gender have to do with group IQ? Woolley and her colleagues surmised that groups with more women are smarter because women tend to be more socially sensitive than men. Thus, the gender factor is real but indirect—that is, it's *mediated* by the property of social sensitivity.

In another classic experiment, group intelligence was measured by presenting small groups of executives with a hypothetical wilderness survival problem. All-female teams arrived at better solutions (as judged by wilderness experts) than all-male teams. The women's collective problem-solving capabilities were enhanced by their collaborative style, while the men's efforts to assert their own solutions led them to get in each other's way. The difference in collective intelligence did not occur because the individual women were smarter than the individual men, but rather because of a difference in gender-related group dynamics (Lafferty & Pond, as cited in Loden, 1985).

Others emphasize creating collaboration to build collective intelligence. Don Tapscott and Anthony D. Williams (2008) promote four elements to develop collective intelligence: openness, "peering" (allowing members to adapt and build on one another's ideas), sharing ideas, and acting globally to access ideas.

ENHANCING GROUP INTELLIGENCE

Woolley and her colleagues surmise that it is easier to raise the intelligence of a group than the intelligence of individuals. Raising group intelligence is not a limited undertaking. I believe from experience and information across many fields of thought that some common factors exist that will help raise group IQ.

Focus on Real Collaboration

Strengthen the group's collective intelligence with norms. Collaboration enhances the group's collective intelligence. Groups whose members align their efforts rather than pursue their own agendas for individual status are able to create higher collective intelligence and produce better outcomes. Focus on the following.

Allowing for Information Sharing

Any information from group members should be considered simply as potentially useful data. Members of effective groups consider all information that may be presented.

Listening to One Another

Maximizing collective intelligence depends on a group's ability to accept and develop "The Golden Suggestion." The Golden Suggestion is any input from any member. The group's collective intelligence is limited when the group allows input only from select individuals or filters Golden Suggestions without allowing the member to fully develop the idea. Research has proven that groups in which even the smartest person in the room dominates the conversation are not very intelligent groups.

Using Dialogue

Dialogue is not used to make decisions but is a free flow of ideas that allows all members of the group to be heard. In dialogue, each person's comments stimulate others' creativity and lead to better responses. The ability of group members to build on one another's ideas and thoughts enhances the individual's thoughtfulness and the group's intelligence. More on the important differences between dialogue and discussion is presented later in this section of the book.

Allowing Constructive Critiques

Constructive critiques emphasize the first part of the phrase rather than the latter. Constructive criticism is *never* aimed at an individual, nor does it criticize or judge a person. The emphasis is on the idea or the process and concrete ideas for improvement.

All of these efforts enhance group members' ability to collaborate and to allow all members to participate in the group's deliberations, to share in the work.

Construct Diverse Groups

Collective intelligence increases as groups creatively and constructively include diverse relevant viewpoints, people, and information in collective deliberations. Groups that integrate the diverse gifts of their members enhance their collective intelligence. When the group feeds fragmentation and opposition, it becomes stupid.

In one situation with which I am familiar, a board that had been used to having complete unanimity of opinion, dominated by the board president, found itself after a couple of years with several new members who had a dissenting viewpoint. The furor that erupted when these members presented a different opinion of a situation seen from their fresh perspective caused an uproar that led the first group of board members to declare the board "broken" and drum up support for a recall election of the new board president. Community opinion was sufficiently swayed by half-truths and innuendos about the "broken" board that the recall was successful. The new board members resigned en masse in protest, and the board was left once again with members who all shared the same opinions—or if they didn't, never said so. I fear that this board's future decisions will not be in the organization's best interest because board members refuse to allow any diversity of thought.

Interestingly, research on what constitutes a diverse group has found that the difference to group IQ comes not from diversity in individual intelligence or gender, nor from racial, ethnic, or cultural backgrounds. It is differences in backgrounds and life experiences that create better working groups (Page, 2007). For example, having all members of a group from middle class backgrounds, whatever race they may be, does not create the divergent perspectives that bring a group new ideas.

Page and economist Lu Hong constructed a mathematical model showing that diverse groups of problem solvers outperformed groups of the brightest individuals—diversity trumped ability—because, he says, diverse members bring different problem-solving skills to the table. Page identifies the following dimensions of diversity:

- Cognitive differences in perspective (different ways of representing situations and problems)
- Interpretation (putting things into different categories and classifications; for example, I may be categorized by different individuals as a facilitator, a former school administrator, an author, a grandfather, or . . .)
- Heuristics (different ways of generating solutions)
- Ways of approaching problems (analyzing a situation, looking for themes)

When members of a group have diverse sets of mental tools, the process of group decision making is less likely to get stuck on suboptimal solutions, and more likely to result in superior ways of doing things.

Include Members With Higher Social Sensitivity

Social sensitivity can be measured. One measure of social sensitivity, developed by Simon Baron-Cohen, a professor of developmental psychopathology at the University of Cambridge, is the "reading the mind in the eyes" test. Google has numerous results that allow users to take the test online and receive instant feedback. One such site is http://glennrowe .net/BaronCohen/Faces/EyesTest.aspx.

ONE WARNING

Groupthink Is Not Group Intelligence

Processionary caterpillars feed on pine needles. They move in a line, each one's head fitted against the rear end of the one in front, foraging for food in the trees.

Jean Fabre, a French naturalist, experimented with a group of the caterpillars, enticing them to the rim of a large flowerpot where he succeeded in getting the first connected with the last one, forming a complete circle which started moving around in a procession which had no beginning or end.

Fabre expected that the caterpillars would recognize the repetition of the landscape after a while and stop, or one rebel would break the line and start the march in a new, more fruitful direction. That's not what happened.

The caterpillars kept marching along, head to butt, continuing to follow the trail and their peers for seven days and seven nights, ultimately succumbing to exhaustion and starvation. Food was nearby and visible, but it was outside the circle the caterpillars had formed. Not one was willing to break the procession, but continued blindly following the insect in front of it along the now-familiar path (Fabre, 1916).

It is up to members to overcome individual biases, to recognize the familiar in the landscape, and to keep from endless nose-to-tail marching into exhaustion.

RESEARCH ON INTELLIGENCE

In a 2010 article in *Discovery News*, Jessica Marshall sums up the key points of recent research on group intelligence:

- The intelligence of teams can be measured using similar methods to testing individuals' intelligence.
- The intelligence of the group's individual members does not matter much in predicting the intelligence of a group.
- Groups where members participated more equally and had more social sensitivity were more intelligent.

One could categorize the abilities of successfully high IQ groups into three Cs—communicating, collaborating, and commiserating (empathizing). When members communicate well, they can collaborate. Groups with members who are socially sensitive (able to commiserate, or empathize) are more intelligent.

Groups' collective intelligence is important to successful outcomes. The group's ability to create a connectedness among its members and be open to creativity, to respect and honor the individual parts while expecting a higher outcome from the whole, is essential to the ability of the group to work well. In smart groups, members are like tuning forks. What sets off a vibration in one creates a resonance in the rest.

Next, we consider the ways that groups talk in order to raise collective IQ, affect the ways they work, and change individuals' mental models.

6

Learning the Ways Groups Talk

In the best of schools, leaders focus collaborative efforts on student learning. With that thought in mind, a high-performing suburban district recently decided that teachers would work for one afternoon twice each month in professional learning teams. The administration announced to the community that all students would be dismissed two hours early on designated Wednesdays, an unpopular move with parents. Teams of teachers got together at the specified times, working in grade-level or subject-area groups. However, teachers were given no orientation for how to talk with one another or focus their conversations.

Seven months later, when I was contacted, many teams were struggling. When I visited first at the school, many teachers couldn't explain any outcomes of the group work. One team was working on common assessments for the department. Another team at the school had spent the time creating a list of goals. One team held up a small triangle that teachers had cut out of a piece of paper and said it was the result of their work time, but did not explain how the diagram related to any effects in the classroom. Parents and teachers were frustrated. The future of the shared time was in question as the community's wait-and-see willingness to support the early release time waned.

These educators had good intentions. They were smart people. They had time and resources, yet many were floundering. Why?

The district in the example asked teachers to collaborate and work together regularly without providing professional development in collaborative skills or creating clear intentions for the work. Student improvement was, of course, the goal, but how does collaborative work help teachers reach that goal?

The school leadership established structures, time for the groups to collaborate, and a menu of tasks on which to work. These are valuable resources to help meet goals, but none prepare teachers for the intricacies of collaborative work. None of them answer the questions group members will have concerning what to do first; how much time to spend developing, implementing, or assessing goals; and how to decide where to focus their energy. An administrator could provide teams with an agenda of tasks and processes that would answer these questions, save time, get faster focus, and help teams work more expediently. But giving people a prescription for work violates the very essence of collaboration—productive invention.

When administrators, teacher leaders from the learning teams, and I began to discuss the district's purpose and goals, the administrative team was able to clarify its intention—to have teachers make instructional decisions based on systematic inquiries into the relationships between teaching and student learning. The intention is broad, but clear enough to help teams make decisions about how and where members should focus their energy.

This is job-embedded professional development supporting continuing cycles of improvement in which the constant focus of conversations is student work and learning events.

Clarity around the guiding purpose for the work is the first element of maintaining focus. When the purpose is clear, groups that refer regularly to the intention can help keep discussions relevant and make decisions about what action steps to take. Group members use agreed-upon meeting standards, well-defined agendas, and clear roles as supports for their work, but a clear guiding purpose is essential.

Maintaining focus also requires that group members pay attention to ways of talking. Two of the most valuable skill sets a group can have are facility with two ways of talking (dialogue and discussion) and understanding of the *seven norms of collaboration*: pausing, paraphrasing, posing questions, placing ideas on the table, providing data, paying attention to self and others, and presuming positive intentions. Why are these tools so important?

DIALOGUE OR DISCUSSION

Group talk is the organizing ingredient of shared learning. How we talk says much about who we are and how effective we can be. Groups that seek to work efficiently and effectively need members who understand how and when to make decisions through discussion—and when to explore an issue in dialogue.

When these distinctions are not clear, the group may experience confusion, tension, and chaos. One elementary school's committee, for example, had long had a tradition of hiring a performing group each spring that would entertain the student body with a different art form. Each year, staff would discuss the theme for the year. One year was ballet, the next a one-act play, another a storyteller, and so on. Each performance was linked directly to a literacy standard.

Eventually, some committee members changed. The time came to move ahead with the tradition, and the item was put on the agenda. A new member who had researched the cost decided to raise the issue and suggested that in the face of ever-diminishing resources, the money might be put to better use. She suggested using the money to purchase classroom sets of books. She called for the group to make a decision to cancel plans for the artist-in-residence.

If not for the extreme upset that resulted, the use of that money could have remained a topic for genuine discussion. However, the rest of the group pushed back, angrily denouncing the new member and a few supporters of the idea for not understanding the school's traditions. What ensued was neither discussion of the proposed action nor real dialogue about the reasons, but a fracas of head butting that left the committee members feeling tired, resentful, and without the ability to move forward productively.

Had the elementary school committee recognized the difference between dialogue and discussion, rather than continuing on a course leading nowhere, members could have had a dialogue about the artist-in-residence and the assumptions group members had about the benefits and then moved on to a more productive discussion and decision making.

Groups use dialogue to reveal and examine perspectives, explore assumptions, and inquire into the theories underlying proposed actions. In short, dialogue is used to understand. It honors the social-emotional brain, helps build connections, and creates a sense of safety. Once a group has reached some conceptual understanding of goals and assumptions regarding the two proposals, efficient discussion can take place. Discussion is used to make a decision.

WHAT IS DIALOGUE?

Dialogue is at the root of all effective group action.

—Edgar Schein

Dialogue is a particular form of communication in schools that precedes and makes possible sound decisions that stay made. It can be transformational in its effect on relationships, school culture, and productivity. It requires skills that, once learned, can and should be naturally applied in all aspects of professional work.

(Continued)

(Continued)

Dialogue is a reflective learning process in which group members seek to understand one another's viewpoints and deeply held assumptions. The word dialogue comes from the Greek *dialogos. Dia* means "through" and *logos* means "word." During this meaning-making process, group members inquire into their own and others' beliefs, values, and mental models to better understand how things work in their perceptions of school goals, challenges, opportunities, and solutions. In dialogue, listening is as important as speaking. For skilled group members, much of the work is done internally. (Garmston & Wellman, 2009)

Dialogue creates an emotional and cognitive safety zone in which ideas flow for examination without judgment.

In dialogue, members work to understand one another's viewpoints. Dialogue requires

- *Listening*—not preparing an argument for the speaker or silently cataloguing all the related information we possess, but listening without carrying on an internal dialogue;
- Developing *shared understanding*—honoring one another's assumptions, agreeing to believe the others' intentions are for the good and not second-guessing motives; and
- Committing to *being open*—allowing for the possibilities within the communal thought.

Dialogue leads to understanding. Discussion leads to decisions.

Mindful group members pay attention to three essential elements during productive dialogue. They monitor themselves, the process of the dialogue, and the new whole that is emerging within the group.

ATTRIBUTES OF
DIALOGUE AND DISCUSSION

	DIALOGUE	DISCUSSION
Definition	Dialogue is a reflective learning process in which group members seek to understand each other's viewpoints and deeply held assumptions (Garmston & Wellman, 1999, p. 55).	Discussion is an act of consideration or examination by argument or comment, especially with the purpose of exploring solutions.
Action	Different views are presented as a way of discovering new views.	Different views are presented and defended in search of the best view to support a decision.
Purpose	To explore complex and subtle issues To practice deep listening To deepen understanding	To analyze and dissect an issue from many viewpoints To have one's view prevail To make decisions
Root	Greek *dia-*, "through," and *logos*, "word"	Latin *discussus*, "to break up"

Michael Dolcemascola, codirector of the Center for Adaptive Schools, and I have described three developmental phases in learning to dialogue (Garmston & Dolcemascolo, 2009). They are *exploring*, *developing*, and *maturing*.

Exploring

People will begin a dialogue using whatever social norms are intact. If a work group has a social norm of attacking others, this will show in early attempts at dialogue. Groups at the developing stage, however, generally have politeness as a norm. When boards of education set aside Robert's Rules of Order to dialogue, their initial interactions may be relatively formal.

At this stage, group members should understand the purposes of dialogue, be able to distinguish dialogue from discussion, and have a conceptual grasp of what it means to set aside internal thoughts that interfere with their ability to understand others. Members may practice exercising the skills of suspension, as well as the response behaviors of pausing, paraphrasing, putting ideas on the table, and inquiring.

A facilitator's tasks at this level, beyond setting expectations for the work, are to start and end the meeting and to see that everyone has a chance to talk. The facilitator mediates and intervenes in attacks.

At beginning group stages, an initial norm is a reluctance to explore differences. When, sometime in a conversation, someone begins to search for differences of opinion and several members try to explore what they are uncertain of or wondering about, a group is beginning to operate at the developing stage.

Developing

At this stage, members begin pausing. Paraphrasing more frequently becomes almost a new social norm. They begin to reveal assumptions. People listen to others, although often the listening may be self-confirming. People become more willing to say what they really think rather than offering what they take to be conventionally acceptable opinions. Instability in the group can emerge as people wrestle over which meaning is more accurate. Leadership is invaluable at this point, and suspension is encouraged.

Group members exercise skills in assuming positive intentions and have internalized the pattern of pausing, paraphrasing, and inquiring. Members are clear about their intentions, choose behaviors congruent with those intentions, and know when to assert themselves and when to integrate with the group's direction. They support the group's purposes, topics, processes, and development.

Maturing

At this phase, curiosity becomes a norm. People identify and publicly explore their assumptions, as if they are removing a veil from themselves and discarding the group rules that have unconsciously governed their beliefs and behaviors. Isaacs, founder of the Dialogue Project at the Massachusetts Institute of Technology, notes that at this stage, people lose the need to have others agree with them or reply in response to their statements. They learn, in a sense, that they are not their point of view but have points of view they can offer to the group for examination. At this stage of development, people stop speaking for others, stop using third-person data about others and situations, and speak more about personal uncertainties, confusions, and curiosities. Isaacs refers to this developmental stage as reflective, characterized by opening up intrapersonal data to the group and withdrawing from consideration ideas previously offered to the group (1999, pp. 242–290).

Also at this stage, members become capable of what Isaacs calls *upstream suspension*—that is, recognizing the sources of thoughts and reactions. This is a transformational stage in dialogue because at this point individuals no longer can maintain the illusion that others are "causing" reactions in them, but understand that they are the source and creator of their own reactions. As a friend of ours says, "I understand you are angry. Of all the possible emotions to select, what led you to select that one?"

Norms of Collaboration

The following social, emotional, and cognitive skills become norms when they reach the status of habits (Garmston & Wellman, 2009). They are the alphabet of professionally productive talk. These skills are not acquired overnight. They demand intention, diligence, and reflection to make them a normal part of educators' talk. Taken as a whole, they are the skills base for social sensitivity and have been found to have a positive effect on a group's capacity to work with cognitively complex situations.

Free norms inventories are available at www.adaptive schools.com. Many groups find these a respectful way to introduce the norms, and then subsequently use them to monitor progress. One useful approach is to select one norm at a time to work on. See *Inventories: Seven Norms of Collaboration & Effective Meetings* on the Adaptive Schools web site (www.adaptive schools.com/inventories.htm) for a norms-supporting tool kit.

Pausing

There is vast research on the positive effects of teacher pausing and silence on student thinking. The "wait time" research of Mary Budd Rowe (1986) has been replicated around the world. By inference, the same applies to adults. Thinking takes time. High-level thinking takes even longer. This research indicates that it takes from 3 to 5 seconds for most human brains to process high-level thoughts. Pausing before responding or asking a question allows time for thinking and enhances dialogue, discussion, and decision making.

Paraphrasing

Use a paraphrase starter that feels comfortable. Begin with "So . . ." or "As you are (verb)ing . . ." or "You're thinking . . .";

then follow the starter with a paraphrase to help others hear and understand one another as they formulate decisions. Paraphrasing is one of the most valuable and least used communication tools in meetings. Even those who naturally and skillfully paraphrase in one-to-one settings often neglect this vital behavior in group settings. Groups that develop consciousness about paraphrasing and give members permission to use this reflective tool become clearer and more cohesive about their work. One caution: don't use the phrase, "I hear you saying" as a starter. That phrase, beginning with "I," is about the listener, not the speaker and often evokes a negative reaction. This form of paraphrasing was taught in the 1960s when it was thought paraphrasing was a language skill. It is not. It is a listening skill.

Posing Questions

Two intentions of posing questions are to explore and to specify thinking. Pose questions to explore perceptions, assumptions, and interpretations, and to invite others to inquire into their own thinking. One recommended practice is to inquire into others' ideas before presenting or advocating one's own ideas. Effective inquiry follows a pattern of pause and paraphrase before posing a question. Humans have a finely-tuned threat mechanism, so offer well-formed questions with a slightly melodic voice rather than in a monotone, and construct questions in plural forms using exploratory language such as: *some, might, seems,* and *possible.* For example, "What might be some purposes of X?"

At times, we question in order to specify thinking. Our brains delete details from streams of data and distort incoming and outgoing messages to fit our own deeply embedded models of reality. This human trait causes difficulties in communication. Conversations go haywire when the various parties make different assumptions about the meanings of words and concepts and neglect to verify or correct their assumptions. Successfully defining and solving problems, and generating solutions, requires specificity. Using gentle, open-ended probes or inquiries beginning with such phrases as "Please say more about," "I'm curious about," "I'd like to hear more about," or "Then, are you saying . . . ?" increases the clarity and precision of the group's thinking.

Five categories of vague speech are worth probing to clarify thinking and communication:

- Vague nouns and pronouns such as *they* or *students*. Press for specificity by asking, Who specifically?
- Vague verbs, such as *understand* or *improve*. Ask what these terms mean.
- Comparatives, such as *better* or *larger*. The issue is: "Better than what?" or "Larger than what?" You must ask to get clarity.
- Rule words, such as *must* or *can't*. What is behind these rules? What are the conditions that make a *must* or a *can't*? Asking questions about rule words may result in learning that the rule was imagined and not real.
- Universal quantifiers, such as *everybody* or *all the time*. Check to see if it really is true for everybody or in all circumstances.

Placing Ideas on the Table

Ideas are the heart of group work. In order to be effective, they must be released to the group. For example, a group member might say, "Here is an idea we might consider. One possible approach to this issue might be . . . ." When individuals indicate ownership of an idea ("I think . . ."), the other group members tend to interact with the speaker based on their feelings for and relationship to the speaker rather than to the idea presented. This is especially true when the speaker has role or knowledge authority related to the topic at hand. To have an idea be received in the spirit in which the speaker intends, the speaker should label those intentions by saying, "This is one idea," "Here is a thought," or "This is not a proposal; I am just thinking out loud."

Knowing when to pull ideas off the table is equally important. For example, say, "I think this idea is blocking us; let's
set it aside and move on to other possibilities." In this case,
continued advocacy of the idea is not influencing other group
members' thinking. This is a signal to pull back and reconsider
approaches.

Consider honeybees as an example. Cornell University
biologist Thomas Seeley (2010) studied the decision making of
swarms that grew too large for their current nest and needed
to find a new home. The queen bee did not make the decisions—the whole swarm did. First, scouts would search out
possible locations. Then, the scout would return to the swarm
and "dance" directions to the new place. The more excited the
scout was about the location, the more the bee would repeat
the dance, emphasizing its point over and over. Other scouts
then would check out the location, and if *they* liked it, would
return to the swarm and do the same dance until all the swarm
was dancing together for the same new spot. Bees don't single-
mindedly stick to an unpopular point of view, according to
Seeley. They simply present their best idea and then let the
group do the work—a "retire and rest" theory, he says, that
may be a neurophysiological approach to consensus making.

Providing Data

Providing data, both qualitative and quantitative, in a
variety of forms, allows group members to develop collective
understanding from their work. Data have no meaning except
that which we make; shared meaning comes from collaboratively organizing, analyzing, and interpreting data. Effective
groups collect and select relevant data for their work, develop
and use data displays, and use data to make decisions. Groups
follow agreed upon protocols and work to invite and sustain
others' thinking through pausing, paraphrasing, and posing
questions.

Group members balance advocacy for their ideas with
inquiry into others' thinking, clarify assumptions, listen

nonjudgmentally, and seek shared understanding. They create an atmosphere of psychological safety and school themselves not to jump to the easiest and quickest solutions but to look beneath the surface for causal factors.

Paying Attention to Self and Others

Attention is the essence of social sensitivity and a key factor in collective intelligence. Meaningful dialogue and discussion are facilitated when each group member is conscious of both self and of others. Skilled group members are aware of what they are saying, how they are saying it, and how others are receiving and responding to their ideas. This includes paying attention to both physical and verbal cues in oneself and others. Since the greatest part of communication occurs nonverbally, group members need to be conscious of the total communication package (Goleman, 2006). Nonverbals include posture, gesture, proximity, muscle tension, facial expression, and the pitch, pace, volume, and inflection in their voices.

Presuming Positive Intentions

Assuming that others' intentions are positive encourages honest conversations about important matters. This is an operating stance that group members must take if dialogue and discussion are to flourish; it is also a linguistic act for speakers to frame their paraphrases and inquiries within positive presuppositions.

Positive presuppositions reduce the possibility that the listener will perceive threats or challenges in a paraphrase or question. Instead of asking, "Does anybody here know why these kids aren't learning?" the skilled group member might say, "Given our shared concern about student achievement, I'd like to examine our assumptions about what might be causing gaps in learning." The first question is likely to trigger defensiveness. The second approach will most likely lead to speculation, exploration, and collective understanding. This is especially true when a speaker has strong emotions about a topic and even more important when the respondent initially disagrees with the speaker.

Assuming that others' intentions are positive promotes and facilitates meaningful dialogue and eliminates unintentional putdowns. Making explicit positive intentions in your speech is one manifestation of this norm.

TEACHER TALK MAKES A DIFFERENCE

Teacher behavior is based on teacher thinking and perceptions. It should be obvious then that teacher talk also is based on teacher thinking. To change behavior, change talk. To change the ways teachers talk, change thinking. The research presented in the previous chapter shows that groups can handle more cognitively complex tasks when members have social sensitivity and turntaking norms and that they are more successful when there is more positivity than negativity, inquiry than advocacy, and focus on other rather than self.

Making day-to-day interactions within teams more positive than negative helps to achieve a productive balance between the team's focus on itself and on its environment and between seeking understanding and asserting authentic beliefs and opinions. A shift in the pattern of discourse leads to measurable success and added value for the organization.

Transforming cultures into positive realms is not easy. Humans are built to interpret events negatively, a hardwired attribute that Seligman (1993) says may be "a legacy from our ancestors thousands of years ago who were well served by remembering—and learning from—negative experiences they had with predators." Although this may have helped our ancestors survive, the tendency can make the modern teacher prone to interpret questionable behavior negatively. Clear discourse can help groups avoid questionable interpretations of others' behavior.

7

Challenging
Mental Models

Agroup of seventh-grade teachers had been meeting regularly since the beginning of the academic year, spending an hour and a half every other week during team time to talk about their students. The principal of this high-poverty school had staked her credibility with her superiors on the idea that the additional professional learning time would help turn the building's low achievement around. I spent our initial session listening in on this group's work.

"Miriam is *such* a problem," a teacher said about a student. "She just *never* stops talking. And Akin—he can't sit still. Even when I can get him to sit at his desk for 10 minutes, I walk over there and he's not paying attention *at all*; he's just doodling all over the desk!" Another chimed in, shaking her head and tsk-tsking. "I have the *same* problem. And Akin's mother is no help at all. She doesn't even show up at parent conferences."

Their sessions had degenerated into a litany of complaints from one or another teacher about this child or that one; rather than focusing on meaningful student work or creating common assessments, potentially significant discussion time had turned into a gripe session. Some teachers stuck to a stony silence with their arms folded, having mentally checked out; others were frustrated and let their frustration be known in various verbal and nonverbal ways. The gripers dominated the group airtime. After the first meeting, I learned from talks with individual teachers that some who had been on friendly terms now were turning against one another. The sense of being a team obviously was fraying.

A fundamental problem was the teachers' underlying and unstated beliefs about their students, learning processes, and their own efficacy. The mental models they held focused on deficiencies, not sufficiencies. A second problem was that the teachers focused on the difficulties in the existing condition rather than mentally envisioning desired states. Unconscious perceptions were shaping their interactions—and most importantly, their effectiveness. Only by reflecting on and surfacing assumptions and beliefs can they begin to change mental models and change outcomes.

WHAT ARE MENTAL MODELS?

Mental models are unconscious explanations of how things work in the real world. They are informed by beliefs, assumptions, and the resulting perceptions, and have explanatory power regarding why things work the way they do and how to improve them. One common mental model of how a telephone works is that I dial a number, the phone rings on the other end, a person answers, and we talk. This model is sufficient for me to use a telephone even though it is inaccurate. The ringing I hear is not coming from the other phone. A mental model may be a script, an image, a set of assumptions, or a controlled vocabulary, or some combination of these elements. "A grown person has tens of thousands of beliefs, organized somehow into a unified system, and generally highly resistant to change," concluded psychologist Milton Rokeach (1964).

Consider this often-repeated story that I heard from Bill Sommers, colleague, high school principal, and professor who teaches aspiring administrators: A research lab put five gorillas into a cage in a study of how rewards and punishment affect gorilla behavior. Inside the cage was a stairway that led to some bananas. One gorilla started up the stairs and received an electric shock, which triggered a spray of cold water on the others. A second gorilla started for the bananas, was shocked, and the group was sprayed again. The pattern repeated when a third gorilla went up. This time, the group beat the gorilla who had attempted to reach the fruit. A fourth gorilla started for the stairs, a fight erupted, and this gorilla also was stopped by the others.

How would these experiences affect new group members? To test this question, researchers replaced a veteran gorilla with a newcomer. The new gorilla tried the stairway, but the others stopped it. A second new gorilla replaced another veteran with the same results. Finally, all five gorillas had been replaced with other gorillas, but the mental models and behaviors formed from the early experiences persisted.

This group had age, but not maturity. This story, true or not, illustrates patterns that occur within groups. Dominant mental models about ways of being, norms of problem solving, and degrees of collective efficacy prevail even when the group's membership changes and environmental conditions shift. I've often wondered what might have happened if one gorilla had initiated some thinking about the problem of reaching those bananas. If that group still doesn't have any bananas, some group development even now might still improve its functioning.

Uncovering Mental Models

Mental models can evolve over time. A categorical programs advisor in a Los Angeles elementary school wrote to me:

> I am a teacher in a nonclassroom position, and I have taken a leadership role in my school for the past five years. During this time, my school (for various reasons) has reached Program Improvement Year 5+. This has caused the school's climate and morale to decline. Although we speak of the importance

of being a body of collaborative professionals, I do not see much evidence of that. In fact, in a recent teacher survey, teachers expressed that there is a lack of trust in the school. This has resulted in a cause-and-effect, nonending battle . . . . Slow academic achievement causes low morale, and a low morale and tension-filled school climate is impacting academic achievement. I was thinking of ways to break this destructive cause-and-effect cycle, but I was lacking fundamental principles. I took advantage of an Adaptive Schools Professional Development workshop and learned to build my skills as a leader. I also learned techniques on how to begin to foster collaboration and a professional community in order to reenergize ourselves and become effective in order to increase student achievement.

In a recent staff meeting, I introduced the seven norms of collaboration and the five energy sources: efficacy, craftsmanship, flexibility, consciousness, and interdependence. Based on teachers' evaluations, they want to learn more about the norms and states of mind, and like one teacher stated, "We are ready and need a change."

I am looking forward to continue implementing the techniques I've learned and to see my school become an adaptive, collaborative, effective school with professionals that are committed to student achievement. (Suzanne Vega, personal communication, 2011)

CHANGING MODELS

To change our working patterns, we first change our mental models. The process requires courage—and time. Educators are often so overwhelmed with increasing day-to-day demands that finding either is difficult. But without these steps, improvement cannot happen.

Growth and change require disequilibrium. We do not learn or move forward when we are in a balanced state. Understanding comes from actively constructing meaning, which depends on the group generating and evaluating information.

Effective groups create safe environments that allow people to take risks and courageously state their assumptions, stretch their imaginations and cognition, research alternatives, and experiment.

We are mostly unaware of the mental models that govern our behavior.

The capacity to create systemic improvement requires examining our organizational and personal mental models. Unchallenged mental models cause us to see the way we have always seen, approach work in the manner we always have, and act fundamentally in the ways we always have acted, which is tantamount to Einstein's definition of insanity—doing the same thing again and again but expecting different results.

Humans don't learn from experience but from reflecting about experience. Publicly examining mental models requires psychological safety. Learning out loud, in public, is strenuous work to understand others and ourselves without judging. We do this best in a spirit of inquiry. The right attitude and environment ready the group for this kind of growth.

EXAMINING PERCEPTIONS

All groups possess collective mental models. Some teams harbor unstated tensions related to these models. These can be identified by listening to group members gathered in corners in the teachers lounge or in the parking lot discussing a meeting—an unproductive way of dealing with issues. However, when group members work together to identify unstated perceptions, they can address the tensions and improve group performance and satisfaction. Discussing uncomfortable issues releases tensions and creates productive interactions and better ways of working.

The consequences of emotional reactions often have long-lasting effects. In one district, a long-term superintendent had a contentious relationship with the head of the teachers association. In the last decade before the superintendent retired, the teachers' contract expired before an agreement was reached each of the three times it came due. A decade and two superintendents later, with a different association leader, the wariness between the district and union continued. Despite shared goals for a high-achieving district and satisfied employees, the emotional pattern had been laid down and had not been changed.

DEEP AND SURFACE STRUCTURE

The Deep to Surface Structure (see Figure 7.1) has its genesis in the work of Noam Chomsky, who in the 1950s and 1960s established the transformational model in linguistics. Richard Bandler and John Grinder elaborated on this work for therapy in *The Structure of Magic,* published in 1975. Since then, applications of this "iceberg" model have been developed in such diverse fields as cognitive behavioral therapy and architecture. Art Costa and I adapted it for training leaders in Cognitive Coaching.

What is the relationship between deep structure and surface structure? Anything that appears in surface structure—by which we mean what people say, what people do, policy statements that are written—are surface manifestations that reveal some meaning and values from the deep structure. Linguistically, everything in surface structure has a corresponding entity in deep structure, and the deep structure elements are the fullest linguistic representations of the individual's experience. What appears on the surface is always an incomplete representation of that experience. A facilitator, through paraphrasing and inquiring, causes a fuller surface structure representation of that which lies below. Only what is given in surface form can be mediated. Facilitators pose mediative questions that serve this function. *Who are "we"?* and *Why are we doing this, and why are we doing it this way?* are examples of questions that reveal mental models held in deep structure.

Certain facilitation strategies or protocols can illuminate mental models, identities, beliefs, and values. In "Changing Mental Models: HR's Most Important Task," author Jeffrey Pfeffer describes an activity done in pairs. One person tells the other a story about a real, work-related incident in which the storyteller felt like a victim—the person was unhappy about what happened and there was little or nothing that could be done about it. The teller makes the story as convincing as possible, so the listener believes the story and feels the emotion involved. Then roles are reversed, and the partner tells his or her "victim" story to the other person (Pfeffer, 2005).

Participants process the experience with questions: What does it feel like to be a victim? What are the advantages and disadvantages of the victim role? Pfeffer notes that "one advantage of being in a victim role is that one gets sympathy, and, in fact, we often see people in subunits who bemoan their shared and unfortunate fate with each other, thereby building social solidarity." The next step in the mindset change process is to have each partner tell the same story he or she just told a partner, but now try to imagine what it would be like to be more in control or more responsible for what transpired. Being in control does not mean things would have turned out perfectly—organizations are interdependent systems, and it is unreasonable to expect to get one's own way.

Pfeffer stresses that the responsibility mindset is simply seeing oneself as an actor affecting, or trying to affect, what goes on rather than being in a more passive role of having things happen. He writes,

> The debriefing continues by having people think about the emotions they experienced with this responsibility mind-set and, again, discussing the advantages and disadvantages of adopting a responsibility mental model. Not everything is great about being responsible; it is, for instance, hard work and can feel burdensome. Feeling responsible also has many positive emotions and advantages associated with it, including feeling more powerful and more connected.
>
> The point of the exercise is not to have people necessarily come to believe one way of thinking is better than another. The objective is to have people recognize that each of us has a choice—or actually a series of choices—we make each day about how we approach the world

and the problems and opportunities it presents to us. We can be victims or responsible. In a similar fashion, we can choose how we view opponents and rivals, and we can choose what assumptions we make and hold about people and organizations and their capabilities and potential. (Pfeffer, 2005)

Correcting behavior at the surface structure level ultimately does not create behavior that is lasting or stays made because—it is just the *tip* of the iceberg. The sources or roots of behaviors live in deep structure, just as in an iceberg only a small part is visible above the surface of the water. The exact amount visible varies from one sixth to one ninth of the whole iceberg. Most of the structure lies underwater, leaving just a fraction available to see.

In this model, *reference structure* contains intense, or "primitive" experiences—the first or earliest of the kind in existence. Examples are one's first kiss, first job, an award given to the school, a hurricane or flood. So reference structure refers to events in the life of an individual or an organization that have the characteristics of being so unique, emotionally impactful, or novel that they become the source of meaning making for the person or the group—most often below the level of consciousness. The contentious relationship between the superintendent and union president lived in the reference structure of the group and permeated perceptions and reactions.

It is out of this reference structure that individuals and groups form beliefs and get a sense of their identity, beliefs, values, and mental models.

The entities in deep structure are defined as follows:

Identity

This is an individual or group's sense of itself; it is related to beliefs and values. This level answers the question "Who am I?" or "Who are we?" For an individual, identity is a framework for understanding oneself. This framework is formed and

Figure 7.1   Deep to Surface Structure

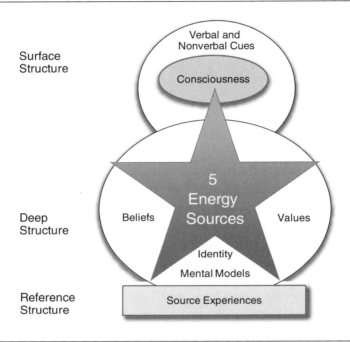

sustained through social interaction. Identity is what makes a person a person; it is the consistently traceable thread that is "me" over time and that distinguishes me from other people or us from other groups.

People construct a set of essential characteristics to define their self-concepts. They interpret experiences and choose behaviors that are intended to maintain the continuity of those self-concepts over time. Group identity is maintained in a similar fashion and is also maintained by comparisons with others. Groups seek positive differences between themselves and other groups as a way of enhancing their own self-esteem. Like individuals, they see themselves as distinct and act as if they were unique.

Albert and Whetten (1985) characterized organizational identity as an evolving answer to a self-reflective question: Who are we as an organization? They concluded that organizational identity could be summarized in three major dimensions: (a) what is taken by the organization to be central to its work, (b) what insiders believe makes the organization distinct from other organizations, and (c) what is perceived by members to be an enduring quality of the organization.

Beliefs

Beliefs are what a group or individual have emotional investment in based on assumptions and convictions that a person holds to be true regarding people, concepts, or things. Teachers who believe that they are more effective are likely to be more effective. When a group believes that its work is manageable, it will enlist the cognitive and emotional resources that allow it to persevere.

Values

Values are either absolute or relative ethical beliefs, the assumption of which can be the basis for ethical action. Values can be defined as broad preferences concerning appropriate courses of action or outcomes. As such, values reflect a group's sense of right and wrong or what ought to be. "Equal rights for all" and "People should be treated with respect and dignity" are representative of values. The most deeply held values are rooted in principles that are grounded in virtue. Principles are universal rules, basic truths, beliefs or laws based on a virtue.

Energy Sources

The energy sources (see Chapter 10) of efficacy, flexibility, craftsmanship, consciousness, and interdependence drive and inspire the hearts and minds of group members, leading them to attain the highest qualities of performance. Consciousness appears in this figure as the link between surface and deep structure, suggesting that through consciousness we access what lies below.

The contentious relationship between the superintendent and association president is an example of processes so intense that they became a part of reference structure, influencing beliefs and attitudes that lived on in deep structure long after the protagonists had left. The relationship between reference structure and deep structure is further illustrated by an example on the individual level given to us by Mary Catherine Bateson, who describes a baby who is fed either on demand or on schedule. The baby having that reference experience with his or her mother will form some impressions—long before speech develops—about the way the world works. The baby's paradigm is that the world responds when I cry for or want for things or the world responds to me on a time schedule (Bateson, personal communication, 1989). That's an oversimplification, but it illustrates how an experience can be so strong that below the level of consciousness, beliefs or mental models are formed about how the world works.

For groups, a teacher strike can be a reference structure experience. Strikes can be divisive, demanding experiences in which a crowd mentality takes over. We know from Elias Canetti's book *Crowds and Power* (1960) that when a crowd is dominated by a single passion, a mood sweeps through the crowd—collective contagion—in which people do and say things that otherwise would be outside of normal behavior. Teachers will do things under those conditions that they otherwise would never consider doing, such as picketing board members' houses, making inappropriate phone calls, or telling students to skip school. These experiences are so emotionally charged that they are imprinted in the memories and the sensory systems of everyone involved.

Such emotionally charged experiences result in mental models being formed. Some mental models might be that administrators are evil, or that teachers are underdogs who need to take care of one another, or that workers and management are natural enemies, or formation of an identity that "we are warriors" who must guard and fight for our rights.

On the other hand, positive reference structures can be initiated in the way illustrated by the principal new to a school whose first act was to interview each teacher asking three questions. "What are you feeling good about here? About what do you have some concerns? What recommendations do you have?" With this administrator, deep structure translations might be *We have a voice here* or *This principal wants to work with us, not over us.*

ILLUMINATING MENTAL MODELS

A number of strategies or protocols can shed light on a group's mental models. Once seen, they can be refined and, with greater consciousness, acted upon. The Card Stack/Shuffle and Assumptions Wall described in Chapter 8 can be used. Other protocols are the Circle Map, Issues Agenda, and the Causal Loop Diagram (Garmston & Wellman, 2009).

Circle Map

One tool that helps groups get past ingrained perceptions is a Circle Map (Hyerle, 2000). The group thinks of an initiative and brainstorms what comes to mind. A recorder draws a circle on chart paper and writes the ideas, using only one color of marker. Members then look at who is in the group and think about who else might have a stake in the initiative but is not represented in the room. All the group members then consider one of those not in the room and brainstorm from that perspective. Their thoughts are recorded in a new color on the chart. The exercise continues until all the essential stakeholder groups have been considered. The result is more data for better planning.

I've seen groups discover they are all middle class and female, serving a poor and multiethnic district. When they begin thinking from the perspective of the people they are serving, they gain new insights.

Issues Agenda

An Issues Agenda helps the group determine the relative importance of issues related to the group's work and provides a visual map to help members record emerging assumptions.

To create an Issues Agenda, each group member uses small sticky note squares to respond in four or five words per note to questions such as:

- What do you think are the most important issues?
- What ideas do you have?
- What do you think might hold the group back from achieving the goal?

Members then post the notes on the wall sequentially and take turns explaining their reasoning. As the group discusses the notes, members begin to move the notes into clusters. They then name the clusters and identify the most important issues.

Causal-Loop Diagram

A Causal-Loop Diagram displays multiple cause-and-effect loops. Group members use square sticky notes to make individual notes about what the group may want to improve and possible factors that are contributing to the lack of success.

The group posts the notes on the wall, and members look at relationships among the items. The group works collaboratively to cluster the notes and identify cause-and-effect loops. Often, the clusters will reveal that cause and effect are not linear. The visual reminder can help members focus on underlying issues and find more effective, less surface strategies to reach a goal.

For example, a group discussing ways to improve math scores might first consider adding time for math instruction, drilling students on math facts, or pulling out students for added instruction. The underlying issues may be quite different and may not be affected by any of those strategies.

Patterns that emerge from these protocols and from Pfeffer's Responsibility Mindset Pairs activity will help group members identify mental models driving their work. Illuminating the mental models in these ways results in safe conversation that brings them into surface structure where they can be examined and modified.

In *The Power of Impossible Thinking: Transform the Business of Your Life and the Life of Your Business* (Yoram, Crook, & Gunther, 2005), the authors advise that when group members face a new decision or challenge, they consider whether they have the correct model to address it. They advise asking

- How does the current model limit or expand the scope of actions?
- Should the model be updated to fit the current environment? What are the risks?
- What old models might apply to the current challenge?
- How can we see the issue at both a macro (forest) and micro (trees) level? Can we examine details first, and then zoom out to the big picture?
- What experiments could we design and test based on hypotheses from our new mental models?

RESULTS

Our mental models can expand or limit our view of possibilities. Our mental models create or limit possibilities by shaping our actions and reactions. Research increasingly supports what we know intuitively—we each see the same event or circumstance through unique lenses.

In the example at the opening of the chapter of the teachers talking, some mental models at work may be a belief that a child's home life predetermines the child's success in school, that stillness is the main indicator of attention, that multitasking precludes learning, that children who talk in class do not respect authority. In this school, the year had disintegrated into rumor, gossip, acrimony, and bad feelings.

Group members used an assumptions wall (Chapter 8) and began to examine their hidden assumptions. Once group members were able to redirect their focus on the right work, they were able to develop some concrete, helpful goals and move toward more effective collaboration.

This group was back on track.

8

Working With Conflict

M ichael Doyle and David Strauss, authors of *How to Make Meetings Work,* tell a story that happened early in their career. They were to facilitate in a conflict between two groups in San Francisco's Chinatown. The issues were intense, and they made three attempts to schedule a meeting between the two groups before both managed to arrive on the same night. Once assembled, Doyle and Strauss made an agonizing discovery. The members of the two groups spoke Chinese, and Doyle and Strauss did not. They decided to facilitate the work through two bilingual attorneys. They instructed the attorney for Group A to have his group describe the problem while Group B listened without interrupting. They repeated the instruction to the attorney for Group B. Next they had the attorney for Group A have his group describe what they thought would be a desired solution. They repeated the instruction to the attorney for the other group. Step by step, the two facilitators guided the groups through a sequence of problem-solving steps. Emotions ran high. The meeting went on into the wee hours of the morning. Finally the two groups came to a solution satisfactory to them. To this day, neither Doyle nor Strauss know what problem they helped the groups solve.

This story sets the stage for four understandings related to groups and conflict. First, the facilitator's contribution is information about process, not content. Second, conflict in the workplace is inevitable. Third, group members, and especially facilitators, need skills in managing themselves in the emotionally charged atmosphere of contention. And finally, groups need models for working with conflict.

CONFLICT'S FORMS AND ROLE

Contention is necessary for sound decision making. Graham (2007) observes,

> Purposeful conversations about curriculum and instruction inevitably evoke deep-held beliefs and philosophies . . . that will vary across a faculty. When differing opinions are brought out into the open, contention will arise. It is at this point that the successful leader must walk a tight line, encouraging staff members to address contention and work through it, while recognizing the emotional toll that disagreements can take. Betty Achinstein (2002) notes that collaboration and attempts at consensus actually generate tension and conflict. Using case studies from two very different schools, she shows that when teachers enact reforms in the name of community, what often emerges is conflict. Whether dealing with teacher collaboration or meeting the needs of a diverse population, conflict within professional communities reflects important differences of beliefs and practices. Her book reframes conflict as constructive when the right tools are used.

Work by Allen Amason and his colleagues (1995) classifies two types of conflict in groups. In affective conflict, personalities become involved, feelings run high, and differences in views become personal. Cognitive conflict is about differences regarding ideas, concepts, and approaches. The most effective groups engage in cognitive conflict but avoid affective conflict.

C-Type Conflict (Cognitive)

Cognitive conflict involves disagreements about substantive differences of opinion. It improves team effectiveness and produces better decisions, increased commitment, increased cohesiveness, increased empathy, and increased understanding. Dialogue is often the medium of choice for fully exploring such differences.

As long as the disagreements among team members focus on substantive, issue-related differences of opinion, they tend to improve team effectiveness. Such cognitive conflict is a natural part of a properly functioning team. C-type conflict occurs as team members examine, compare, and reconcile these differences. It requires teams to engage in activities that are essential to a team's effectiveness. It focuses attention on the all-too-often ignored assumptions that may underlie a particular issue.

Many beginning groups that have not reached higher levels of effectiveness or maturity believe conflict must be avoided at all costs and that any conflict is not productive. As Amason et al. (1995, p. 29) say, "The problem is that, once aroused, conflict is difficult to control."

A-Type Conflict (Affective)

Disagreements over personalized, individually-oriented matters reduce team effectiveness. Affective conflict lowers team effectiveness by fostering hostility, distrust, cynicism, avoidance, and apathy among team members. This type of conflict focuses on personalized anger or resentment, usually directed at specific individuals rather than ideas. It often emerges when C-type conflict becomes corrupted because members lack the skills or norms to disagree gracefully. In such settings, disagreement about ideas can become personalized.

Under these conditions, not only does the quality of solutions decline, but commitment to the team erodes also because its members no longer identify themselves with the team's actions. The result is a downward spiral of reduced effectiveness. As we have seen in Chapter 5, too often this leads to teams with more negativity than positivity in their interactions.

Destructive conflict produces poorer decisions, decreased commitment, and decreased cohesiveness. Teams that can use C-type conflict without generating A-type conflict develop abilities that other teams do not have. Teams that use the seven norms of collaboration and use strategies to talk about difficult topics successfully engage in cognitive disagreements without personalizing them.

Groups with no cognitive conflict tend to make decisions based on the loudest voices, or the leader's sentiments. Decisions made this way tend to be low-quality and get little commitment or follow-through.

So, the experts say, conflict is inevitable, even desirable. The emotional baggage we bring to conflict renders it more daunting than it need be. Conflict, says aikido master Thomas Crum (1997), is just energy in the system, neither good nor bad. It is we who bring unpleasant concepts to it. Treat your opponent respectfully, Crum says, not trying to harm him; rather, use his energy for your aims. Paraphrasing, as described in Chapter 6, is a potent verbal form of aikido. It does not resist the energy emanating from another, but flows in the direction of the other person's force.

MODELS FOR WORKING WITH CONFLICT

The opening story about the conflict in Chinatown underscores the point that those working to solve a conflict do not need to know the content of conversations; rather, they are there to be process experts. Many models of conflict resolution exist. Older models encourage spending time defining the problem, its sources, and its causes. More recently, this approach is being set aside because it buries people in the emotional baggage

related to the problem, actually making members less resource-
ful than if they were to focus instead on the desired state and
the resources necessary to get there. Chip and Dan Heath (2010)
describe an approach used by solutions-focused therapies
in which a "miracle question" is asked: "Suppose you could
go to bed and wake up tomorrow morning and this problem
would be completely resolved. What is the first small sign
you would see that would tell you that the problem is gone?"
In one group I worked with, their answer was that the group
members would trust each other. Notice that this is a start in the
right direction, but needs specifics. "What will you see and hear
when you are trusting each other?" I asked. This question produced a list of specific, observable behaviors the group could
work toward and measure.

This approach works on what the Adaptive Schools and
Cognitive Coaching communities call a Desired State Map.

In working with this map, the first step is to describe the
desired state. If a group's members have been working at
cross-purposes, the desired state is that they are cooperating.
Cooperating needs to be defined, so the most important work is
to list the indicators of cooperation. What would participants
see and hear that would signify cooperation?

The next step is to identify resources needed to attain
that desired state. We think of resources as skills, knowledge,
attitudes, or energy sources. (Energy sources are described in
greater detail in Chapter 10.)

Figure 8.1   Desired State Map

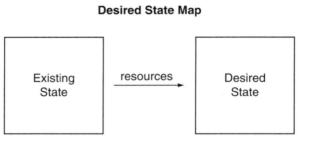

The most important resources are always internal, as are assumptions, beliefs, and the values that drive our thinking but are rarely expressed for others to hear.

Two facilitator protocols are useful for surfacing these deeper worlds contributing to conflict: a Card Stack/Shuffle and an Assumptions Wall. Both of these direct the group's conversation beyond mere wants to needs and toward values, beliefs, and identity.

Card Stack/Shuffle

The Card Stack/Shuffle starts with two stem-completions, each written by each person on a separate 3-by-5 card. The stems on the card are "Productive conflict requires . . ." and "During conflict, my tendency is . . . ." The group stacks and shuffles the cards and passes them to one person in a different group who will begin the process. Person A selects a card and reads it out loud. Group members generate possible assumptions related to the response on the card. The process is repeated with other members drawing and reading a card. Next, group members generate possible implications of those assumptions. In this way, they safely explore deep structure mental models, identities, beliefs, and values related to the topic. Use stems related to the issue at hand, whether grading, discipline, curriculum, or whatever topic the group needs to examine.

Assumptions Wall

Individuals list their assumptions about a topic, then choose one that most informs their behavior. They write their choice on a sentence strip in 8 to 12 words and post the strip on an Assumptions Wall.

The facilitator models how to inquire about the assumptions using mediational questions (discussed later in this chapter), positive presuppositions, and examples of inquiry questions such as, "What makes this important to you?"; "Is it your sense this is true in all circumstances?"; or "How did you come to feel this way?" Individuals inquire about posted assumptions in round-robin fashion.

As an alternative, have the group list assumptions related to a topic. The group selects one to three assumptions and makes inquiries about these. The group then identifies implications of the selected assumptions.

The assumptions wall process works best with groups of 4 to 12 members. Caution the group not to "beat to death" the first assumption explored, and intervene and correct the group whenever the inquiry begins to sound like interrogation and disbelief.

WHEN CONFLICT IS IRRESOLVABLE

Groups must learn to distinguish between a problem to solve and a polarity to be managed. Polarities are persistent, chronic issues that are unavoidable and irresolvable. How to get students in and out of the cafeteria in a timely manner when there are more students than space is a problem to solve. Balancing the need for personal autonomy and the need to work together as a team is a polarity to be managed.

I am grateful to Carolyn McKanders, codirector of the Center for Adaptive Schools, for teaching me about polarities and giving me permission to use portions of the following skills builder that originally appeared at www.adaptiveschools .com. Polarities are natural tensions that are always present in social systems—friend and partner relationships, marriages, communities, school staffs, work teams, associations, school district offices, departments, and families. Polarities have two or more right answers that are interdependent, and they must be managed by *both/and* thinking. Both/and thinking avoids the polarization involved in beginning a thought with "But . . ." and encourages an inclusive approach. For more, see my article "Use 'both/and' thinking to find the best of two sides of a conflict," in the *Journal of Staff Development* (Garmston, 2008b).

Barry Johnson's work *Polarity Management: Identifying and Managing Unsolvable Problems* (1996) offers a set of principles, tools, and structures for identifying and using the natural tensions created as individuals and organizations attempt to engage in cognitive conflict. These tensions often manifest as *polarities*—ongoing, chronic issues that are unavoidable and unsolvable. Johnson asserts that when groups can distinguish between a problem to solve and a polarity to manage and can effectively deal with both, they are able to celebrate and capitalize on diversity and convert resistance to change to a resource for sustainable strength and adaptivity.

Groups may use a Polarity Map to assist in this work.

THE POLARITY MAP

The Polarity Map is a tool for mapping paradoxes or dilemmas. The map provides a structure for making invisible tensions

---

PROBLEMS AND POLARITIES

Leaders, teams, and organizations need to ask this fundamental question when faced with a challenge: *Is this a problem to solve or is it an ongoing polarity we must manage well?* Problems to solve are those with one right answer (or two or more independent right answers); for example, *How do you spell* acknowledgment? or *What should we include in our parent survey?*

In contrast, polarities to be managed are sets of opposites that can't function well independently. They require *both/and* thinking. Because the two sides of a polarity are interdependent, you cannot choose one as a solution and neglect the other. The objective of managing polarities is to get the best of both opposites while avoiding the limits or downsides of each.

Some examples of polarities to manage are: work *and* home, individual *and* team, stability *and* change, independence *and* interdependence, and planning *and* action.

visible and for addressing the whole polarity picture. Once the map is completed through collaborative conversation, it provides a focus for the group to engage in dialogue from diverse perspectives.

The structure is a square divided into four quadrants. The right and left halves are each called *poles*. The upper part of each pole contains the positive aspects of that pole, referred to as its *upside*. The lower part of each pole contains the negative aspects of that pole and is called the *downside*. For maximum effectiveness in managing a polarity, groups create and discover the content of all four quadrants.

Figure 8.2   Polarity Map

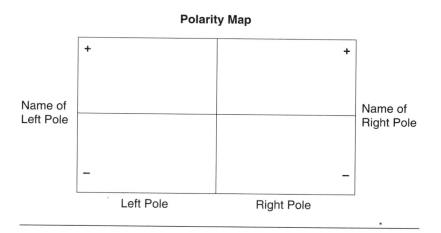

**GUIDELINES FOR
CREATING A POLARITY MAP**

- **Define the challenge.** Identify an ongoing, chronic issue that
  - ☐ Is within your sphere of influence.
  - ☐ Has eluded problem solving.
  - ☐ Must be addressed in the next two months.

(Continued)

(Continued)

- **Identify a key polarity.** A polarity differs from a problem in that all four of the following must be present. Explore these questions to learn if you have a polarity.
  - ☐ In what ways do you continue to experience this issue over time?
  - ☐ In what ways are there two interdependent alternatives? This means that you can only focus on one pole for so long before you are required to focus on the other pole.
  - ☐ What is the necessity of having the upsides of both poles over time?
  - ☐ To what extent will focusing on one upside to the neglect of the other eventually undermine your productivity?

Use dialogue to create a description of the issues that doesn't lay blame, and describe opportunities and polarities present in any given situation. Refer to Chapter 6 for descriptions and tips on using dialogue.

- **Agree on the names for the poles.** Names for poles are value-neutral. Avoid language with charged connotations. One obvious political example of this type of language is the use of terms such as *prochoice, antiabortion,* and *prolife*.
- **Write the pole names on the map.** The map is created on chart paper so that group members may see the map as it unfolds.
- **Brainstorm together the content for each quadrant.**

Aim for four to eight entries in each quadrant. Identify both upsides, asking, "What are some positives or upsides of ____ (this pole)?" Then identify both downsides, asking, "What are the negatives of overfocusing on a pole to the neglect of the other pole?" This order can be modified to meet individual and group needs. The result of the brainstorming is that oppositional values and fears are identified and respected as important.

- **Agree on a higher purpose and a deeper fear.**

Agreeing on a higher purpose and a deeper fear integrates oppositional views and provides a reason to manage the tension between the two views. The higher purpose is the major benefit for managing the polarity well, and the deeper fear is the major negative for not managing the polarity well.

Once a group has completely mapped a polarity on chart paper, a facilitated conversation offers members the opportunity to view and explore the dilemma as a whole and from multiple perspectives. Further, the group can now generate strategies for staying in the upsides of both poles while avoiding the downsides of each pole.

Mediational questions can help promote group dialogue and discussion. These kinds of questions are intentionally designed to engage and transform group members' thinking and perspectives. Mediational questions are invitational in tone and form (Costa & Garmston, 2002, pp. 86–87).

INVITATIONAL QUALITIES OF MEDIATIONAL QUESTIONS

Use an approachable voice. The questioner's voice has a lilt and melody rather than a flat, even tenor.

Use plurals to invite multiple concepts and perspectives:

- What *ideas* do you have?
- What *alternatives* are emerging for us?

Select words that express tentativeness, which invites exploration:

- What conclusions *might* you draw?
- What *hunches* do you have?

Use invitational stems (dependent clauses and prepositional phrases) to enable the behavior to be performed. These stems also employ positive presuppositions, subtle inferences that assume capability and empowerment:

- As you consider . . .
- As you reflect on . . .
- Given your expanded viewpoint . . .

Key Examples of Mediational Questions Related to Polarities

- As you reflect on our collective wisdom, what new learning or insights are emerging for you?
- Given our expanded perspective, what might some benefits be for managing this polarity well? What might some higher purposes be that will benefit all of our students?
- What might some of our deepest fears be if we fail to manage this polarity well?
- As we reflect on phrases in each quadrant, what might be some assumptions, values, or beliefs present?
- Given our desire to stay in the upsides of both poles, what are some strategies?
- What are some indicators that will tell us we are moving to the downside of a pole? Who will remind us and how?
- What seems most important to all of us here?
- What are we learning and noticing about polarities and our work?

- What are some impacts of collaboratively mapping a polarity?
- How might we apply this to other areas of our work?

I invite readers to pursue more detailed descriptions of polarity mapping either in McKanders' work (2009) or in Johnson's (1996) seminal work on this topic.

SECTION III

Developing a Sense of Community

9

Becoming a Self-Directed Group

Group maturity is a matter of learning rather than age. Group members who want to develop a mature group develop their abilities to think, reason, and understand. They develop cognitive skills and become group wise, in addition to working to acquire new subject knowledge and skills. Cognitive complexity distinguishes the good from the extraordinary. Cognition is the mother of behavior; sound thinking results in effective practice.

Expert teachers have a different level of knowledge, efficiency, and insight than novice teachers. (Sternberg & Horvath, 1995) Expert, or mature, groups likewise are more effective in practice. Mature staffs enjoy a high degree of trust with colleagues and leaders. They are more capable of meeting school improvement goals than less mature staffs that have less trust and fewer collaborative skills (Gordon, 2002).

Working groups can take steps to become more mature. Group members who know this see the group not as the group is, but as it might be. While each group is unique, each has the capacity to develop the internal resources, knowledge, and skills for effective, on-target, relevant, and satisfying work.

Mature groups are more likely to be self-monitoring, self-reflective, and self-modifying than novice groups. Without self-monitoring and reflection, a group is doomed to repeat the same unproductive patterns over and over again. The deepest goal of professional learning is to strengthen teachers' individual and collective capacities for continuing their own self-improvement for the benefit of student learning.

THE SELF-DIRECTED GROUP

Groups that work at higher levels of effectiveness cultivate certain habits of learning in group members. Self-directed learners routinely

- *Self-manage.* They are clear about the group's expected outcomes, have a strategic plan, anticipate success indicators, and thoughtfully explore creative alternatives.
- *Self-monitor.* They establish strategies for paying attention to whether the plan is working that also inform decisions about altering the plan.
- *Self-modify.* They reflect on, evaluate, analyze, and construct meaning from their experiences. They apply what they learn to future activities, tasks, and problems (Costa & Garmston, 2002).

Self-Management

Essential to becoming a high-performing group is the group's willingness to agree to the five meeting standards (Chapter 1) and to abide by the seven norms of collaboration (Chapter 6). Achieving expected outcomes requires that group members work together effectively, and the standards and norms provide structures to allow that work to be efficient.

To integrate the seven norms of collaboration into working groups, leaders begin by sharing a rationale for using these practices. Group members assess their use of the norms and select which might be the most productive to develop at the start. Instructions for using the norms inventories are available on the Adaptive Schools website (www.adaptiveschools .com/inventories.htm).

Community groups, too, are interested in self-management and can increase their effectiveness with the seven norms. Wilson High School in Los Angeles, for example, was going through challenges with office space. The coordinator of the Small Learning Communities office offered to share the office with the Parent Center, and together the offices formed what the school calls the Welcome Center. Over time, the Welcome Center developed a role for itself working with parents in both formal and informal settings to support Adaptive Schools applications. When a colleague shared a copy of the seven norms of collaboration in Spanish, a Welcome Center leader eagerly offered to provide a series of one-hour bilingual training sessions for parents and presented mental models of people who embody each of the norms. The parents practiced paraphrasing with a telephone activity to plan an upcoming birthday party. Partner A was the customer and Partner B was the business owner. They laughed about the importance of attentive listening, especially when money is involved. In subsequent conversations, they examined how the norms might look and sound in their daily lives. They role-played conversations with each other to simulate how they might talk with students about the day's learning or other events.

Why do the norms make such a difference for teams? In a study of 60 business teams, Losada and Heaphy (2004) sought to understand how communication practices and emotional dynamics influenced performance levels. They studied positive and negative team communications, inquiry and advocacy, and talking about self as contrasted with talking about others. Teams were rated as high, medium, or low based on sales, customer satisfaction, and observations and interviews by superiors. Interactions were coded as positive if support, encouragement, or appreciation was present and coded negative for disapproval, sarcasm, or cynicism.

In high-performing teams, the ratio of positive to negative was 5.8 to 1. The ratio for the low-performing teams was an astonishing 1 to 3. High-performing teams balanced inquiry and advocacy, while the low-performing teams advocated more than they inquired by a 19-to-1 ratio. (See the table below.) As time went on, high-performing teams flourished and became even more effective, creative, and adaptive. In fact, Losada concludes in a separate study (Fredrickson & Losada (2005, p. 685) that humans flourish when the ratio of positive to negative is 3 to 1 and defines *flourishing* as acting with goodness, generativity ("broadened thought action repertoires and behavioral flexibility"), growth, and resilience. When humans flourish, Fredrickson and Losada continue, they are innovative, highly flexible and stable.

Communication Ratios: High-,
Medium-, and Low-Performing Teams

Success Levels	Positive to Negative	Inquiry to Advocacy	Talking About Self to Talking About Others
High-performing	5 to 1	1 to 1	1 to 1
Medium-performing	2 to 1	2 to 3	2 to 3
Low-performing	1 to 3	1 to 19	1 to 29

Self-Monitoring

Self-monitoring is key for group development. Self-monitoring requires gaining accurate information about performance. The best and most persuasive data come from group members' own reporting and assessment. Since the most motivating information is self-generated, maturing groups should make generating their own data a deliberate goal in professional development.

When teachers have frequent external feedback, they come to rely on that feedback and to depend on others' input to improve. I define feedback as observations from others about one's performance when the information is judgmental ("You made a good synthesis when . . .") or when it comes with advice ("Next time you might consider . . .").

Bruce Joyce and Beverly Showers, who introduced the concept of peer coaching, noted that when feedback is perceived as either good or bad—as evaluative—the effect is negative. "When teachers try to give one another feedback, collaborative activity tends to disintegrate," Showers and Joyce write. "Peer coaches told us they found themselves slipping into 'supervisory, evaluative comments' despite their intentions to avoid them" (1996, p. 15).

Two commonly held myths about feedback are that feedback helps people see themselves more accurately and that feedback improves team effectiveness.

At DuPont and Colgate-Palmolive, members of teams listened to feedback from peers, supervisors, and subordinates about how to be better workers so they could better understand their impact on others and improve their effectiveness working together (Sanford, 1995). In fact, the exact opposite occurred. Feedback undermined these goals and produced negative side effects. DuPont and Colgate-Palmolive changed their organizational commitment to put in place practices that help workers build capabilities for self-reflection and self-assessment.

Sanford concluded that feedback reduces the capabilities of self-reflection and self-assessment, reinforces the pattern that others will and should tell us how we are doing, and reduces our capacity to be self-reflective and self-accountable.

In related work, Sanford reports this truth also holds for 9- and 10-year-olds. At the beginning of a study with 9- and 10-year-old students, most children could not accurately report personal behaviors. They defended their self-observations even when faced with indisputable contradictory evidence such as film and recordings. Group 1 instructors used video and audio recordings to improve the accuracy of the students' observations. Students depended on the recorded material before making their own declaration. Group 2 instructors gave no feedback. They asked each student to reflect on how his or her behavior matched the stated procedure. Group 2 instructors did not correct student perceptions or provide outside evidence. Initially, students' accuracy was very low. After a few weeks, the students' reflections became increasingly accurate.

Praise has always been considered appropriate for shaping some simple learning and behaviors, for working with very young children, or training animals. However, questions linger about using praise as psychological candy. In one classic classroom study, Mary Budd Rowe (1974) found that elementary students who were frequently praised by their teachers showed less task persistence than their peers.

Kohn (1993) reported on two other research studies. One found that praise does not correlate with student achievement gains. The other concluded that correlation between teachers' rates of praise and students' learning gains are not always positive; even when correlations are positive, they are usually too low to be significant.

Similarly, I find in working with adults that the benefit of self-reflection over external feedback also applies in three settings. We have found in Cognitive Coaching seminars that teachers experience as much growth from post-lesson reflections with peers when they have not had an observation as when they have had one. Cognitive Coaching changes teachers' capacity for self-modification. Second, in seminars aimed at developing participants' skills, mediating for self-reflection is producing data, discoveries, and behavior changes. Finally, in work teams, personal reflection followed by mediated conversation with group members has led to rapid improvements in group effectiveness.

Productive group members spend time self-assessing to improve self-management. Productive groups routinely schedule time and plan structures for members to self-reflect. Most groups have more work to do than they have time, yet the only way to improve is through reflection. Contrary to popular belief, we do not learn from experience, only from reflecting on experience.

Groups that are improving commit to a task-to-process ratio, agreeing to set aside time at each meeting to reflect on their work.

Processing time may occur at any point during the meeting. Processing questions directed at thoughts, feelings, and observations are a resource to support self-directed learning. Self-monitoring questions help the group clarify its intentions and help members know when to use a behavior, how much and in what form, when to change a behavior, and how to know one's choice is sound. Focusing on each of these points sharpens behavioral learning. Each can serve as a topic for self-reflective process questions.

Effective groups have facilitators who will pose a question either in the middle of a group's activity or at the end. One generic question is, "What are some decisions we are making about how and when to participate in this meeting?" After group members have time to reflect, they follow up with the answer to the question, "How did those decisions affect you and the group?"

Group members can respond to questions in journals, share their response with a neighbor, or talk together as a group about their reflections. Inevitably, most make more effective choices in the next portion of the meeting, and the group becomes more effective. When the group regularly asks members to reflect in this way, members sharpen their metacognitive skills and the results are improved behavior and team effectiveness.

Another method is to have group members complete a meeting inventory at the end of a meeting. The group distributes a Likert-type scale questionnaire at the end of each meeting. Members rate each item from 1 to 5. The questionnaire can be designed around any principle on which the group is working. Three principles most useful to meeting success are

- Stay on only one topic at a time.
- Use only one process at a time.
- Ensure balanced participation.

Members complete the form and hand it in as they exit the meeting.

The group summarizes and displays the data at the beginning of the next meeting. For the first 5 to 10 minutes of that subsequent meeting, talk about the data. What do group members notice? How does this jibe with an individual's own recollections? What does the data suggest we might give special attention to (be conscious of) in today's meeting? Reach agreement about which areas to particularly attend to, and perhaps share ideas about how to accomplish that goal. Remarkable improvements accrue from this simple procedure. Does it take time? Yes. Does it ultimately save time and make the group more effective? Again, yes. Is it worth the investment? You must answer this. Ask yourself what outcomes you have.

Reflection need not take much time. In fact, many staffs adopt a task-reflection ratio for their meetings in which they agree to spend a specific amount of time at each meeting reflecting on how well they are working together. A friend of mine, Dave Schumaker, when working as a middle school principal, introduced 5 minutes of protected time for journal writing at the beginning of each staff meeting. Initially, teachers groaned. But after awhile, if he overlooked the time, the teachers demanded it.

Self-reflection is most valuable if done regularly, allowing group members to develop, refine, and make habitual their skills of self-observation and analysis. Because educators always have more tasks than time, almost all bright and task-oriented groups resist this notion at first. But, eventually, they realize that any group too busy to reflect about its work is too busy to improve. Reflection creates more permanent change than using process observers or any external rating system.

Meeting Inventory	Strongly Disagree ↓				Strongly Agree ↓
Decide who decides.					
We were clear about our roles in the decision-making process.	1	2	3	4	5
We were clear about the decision-making processes being used.	1	2	3	4	5

Meeting Inventory	Strongly Disagree ↓				Strongly Agree ↓
Define the sandbox.					
We were clear about which issue(s) we explored live in our sandbox.	1	2	3	4	5
Develop standards.					
We adhered to one process at a time.	1	2	3	4	5
We adhered to one topic at a time.	1	2	3	4	5
We balanced participation.	1	2	3	4	5
The degree to which I felt listened to	1	2	3	4	5
The degree to which I listened to others	1	2	3	4	5
We engaged in productive cognitive conflict.	1	2	3	4	5
We were clear about meeting roles.	1	2	3	4	5
Design the surround.					
We managed the environment in a way that supported our work.	1	2	3	4	5

Self-Modification

Like weather systems and national economies, collaborative teams are composed of independent but interrelated elements that make up the whole. They are organized by nonlinear mechanisms that continuously respond to other elements in the system. It is impossible to understand their dynamics using linear logic; instead, we need to use sophisticated nonlinear mathematical models (Losada & Heaphy, 2004). Maturana and Varela (1987) tell us that systems choose what to notice and how to pay attention.

In my experience, the tone and tenor of a group can change in an instant. I have seen groups that were locked in battles transform into a team with the interjection of a simple difference. When one group member asked another for ideas, for example, the person posing the question immediately demonstrated respect for another, and the quality of the group's work escalated immediately. The group's established pattern was disturbed. The two main principles of nonlinear systems were set in motion: Everything affects everything else, and tiny events cause major disturbances.

Group members can create useful disturbances in order to increase the group's effectiveness and improve how the team—the system—attends and responds. Reminding one another of meeting standards, adopting and keeping to the norms of collaboration, and revealing hidden assumptions all help create an atmosphere for change. The norms of collaboration are based on deceptively simple skills: Pausing, paraphrasing, posing questions, providing data, putting ideas on the table, paying attention to self and others, and presuming positive intention. These skills become norms when they become habits. Turning the norms into habits requires group members' focus, mindfulness, and perseverance. Groups that perform well on the five standards for successful meetings (one topic at a time, one process at a time, balanced participation, productive cognitive conflict, and clarity about meeting roles) usually produce maximum work in minimal time with maximum satisfaction.

The collective work of planning, scheduling, problem solving, assessing, refining curriculum, and instruction is the context within which the staff examines itself and commits to improvement.

Using Learning Instruments

Instrumentation is a technique used to facilitate learning by gathering data in a systematic or structured way. Groups can use learning instruments to assess themselves prior to learning a new skill, to activate and engage prior learning, to support learning a new concept, to help in self-reflection, to generate data to uncover group issues and challenges, to inventory group members' knowledge, strategies, and skills, and to summarize and integrate learning. The purpose of a learning instrument is to gather data to stimulate a conversation.

1. Start with clear expectations. To get the maximum value out of an instrument's use, all group members should know and understand why an instrument is being used, how it relates to the larger learning agenda and their jobs, how the results will be used, and anyone to whom the results might be communicated. For example, a leader or facilitator might introduce an instrument by saying, "This is to sample our reactions at this point in time. We will use the results to begin our conversation about the topic."

Group members are silent while everyone works through the instrument. However, waiting for 100% of the group to complete all written work can cause the fast finishers to become restless. The group should be ready to move forward when about 95% are finished.

2. Compose or select the instruments. Groups often are capable of devising their own surveys. Constructing a survey instrument is an art in itself. Numerous small decisions must be made—about content, wording, format, and placement—that can have important consequences.

Writing a question for a survey instrument involves:

- Determining the question content, scope, and purpose;
- Choosing the response format for collecting information from the respondent; and
- Figuring out how to word the question to get at the issue of interest.

Word choice is critical. When devising a survey, test some of the questions with a small group before releasing the instrument. People are sensitive to subtle changes in wording and syntax. Sometimes changing just one word can have a powerful impact. In a famous study done in 1941 and replicated many times, respondents were asked one of two questions,

1. "Do you think the United States should allow public speeches against democracy?"

2. "Do you think the United States should forbid public speeches against democracy?"

Support for free speech was 20% greater for respondents that answered question number 2 (Rugg, 1941).

I suggest that groups interested in devising their own instruments consult some literature for guidelines. One place to start is with a research report (Martin, 2006) from the Census Bureau, *Survey Questionnaire Construction*, available online at www.census.gov/srd/papers/pdf/rsm2006–13.pdf.

A few instruments that combine simplicity with potency are:

- *Self-report inventories.* These inventories can produce information in a structured way about leadership style, cognitive style, educational philosophy, or other personal attributes. The questions are generally forced-choice, rating scales, yes-no, or multiple-choice. As group members score, interpret, and discuss results, they construct personal meaning. See Figure 9.1 for an example of this type of survey. (Costa & Garmston, 2002)

Once groups understand the differences in members' educational beliefs, conversations take on more meaning and conflicts are better understood and diffused. A school board I know used this instrument to inquire about members' views. One result was that meetings became shorter. Board members understood the futility of trying to change another's values, and instead they sought solutions that embraced multiple views.

- *Feedback devices.* Feedback instruments help groups collect data about their behavior in order to develop their skills. Designated members gather data while the group works on a task or conducts a meeting. These "process observers" usually use a form to gather data, and then report the data to the group. The data-gathering form might note the frequency of member contributions during an interchange or require a tally of how often individuals paraphrased one another or asked probing questions for more information.

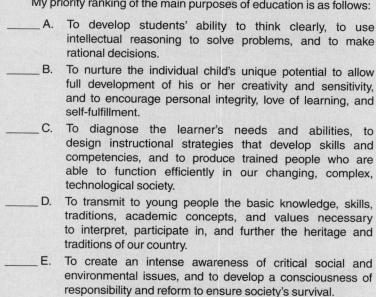

Figure 9.1   Self-Report Inventory on Educational Goals

Educational Goals

In the space provided, rank the following statements from 1 (most important) to 5 (least important) according to your personal priorities and belief systems.

My priority ranking of the main purposes of education is as follows:

_____ A. To develop students' ability to think clearly, to use intellectual reasoning to solve problems, and to make rational decisions.

_____ B. To nurture the individual child's unique potential to allow full development of his or her creativity and sensitivity, and to encourage personal integrity, love of learning, and self-fulfillment.

_____ C. To diagnose the learner's needs and abilities, to design instructional strategies that develop skills and competencies, and to produce trained people who are able to function efficiently in our changing, complex, technological society.

_____ D. To transmit to young people the basic knowledge, skills, traditions, academic concepts, and values necessary to interpret, participate in, and further the heritage and traditions of our country.

_____ E. To create an intense awareness of critical social and environmental issues, and to develop a consciousness of responsibility and reform to ensure society's survival.

Absolutely critical to using feedback devices is ensuring that members understand that the purpose of the instrument is to gather information to inform a conversation to support their self-management. A feedback device is not evaluation. Also critical is how the data are reported. Members need to be shown the data, not told. Sharing data avoids observers' making unintentional value judgments, such as saying, "and there were lots of paraphrases, 13, in fact." Data should preferably be shown using a chart or overhead projector. The process observer leads a conversation using questions such as:

1. What are you noticing?
2. What patterns do you see?
3. What surprises you?

4. Given your assessment of the data, what practices do you think we should continue, stop, do more, do less, or do differently?

- *Conceptual jump starts.* These instruments have simple formats but are complex to construct. A person in charge of a segment of a meeting determines the simplest possible question that will evoke the richest possible reflection. Conceptual jump-start instruments are often best asked of trios or quartets who respond before a full-group conversation.

Bill Baker, a founding colleague of the Cognitive Coaching work gives these examples: "Compare inquiry with interrogation. What is the same? What is different? What are your conclusions?" "How can we use this information in our work with students (or ourselves)?" "Compare praise with reinforcement. In what ways are they the same and different? Under what circumstances do we do each?"

Or individuals could respond to questions such as, "What is the single most important aspect you wish to see in student essays?"

3. Process findings. Instruments are helpful only if the data that result are used well. Groups use personal inventories to articulate insights and build bridges between the personal data and the group's learning task. Groups may spend 10 minutes processing their findings, or with more complex feedback or conceptual jump-starts, they may spend a half-hour on the task. Members look for patterns in their responses, seeking major learnings. Their overarching question is always: What have we learned that helps us improve student learning?

CONCLUSION

The best source of deepening expertise for both teaching and working collaboratively is critical self-reflection. Self-directed learning is an essential attribute for educators. Groups that regularly use the skills of self-managing, self-monitoring, and self-modifying can shift the norms of the culture and the impact of their instruction.

EXPERT GROUPS EXCEED NOVICE GROUPS

In knowledge

Expert groups

- Organize their knowledge more thoroughly
- Integrate knowledge more thoroughly
- Have more complex and interconnected planning structures
- Demonstrate practical knowledge of the social and political context in which their work occurs

In efficiency

Expert groups

- Can do more in less time with less effort
- Use higher-order processes to plan, monitor, and evaluate ongoing efforts to solve problems
- Spend time trying to understand a problem, whereas novices invest more time trying out different solutions
- Are more likely to monitor their solution attempts
- Are more likely to reflect and to learn by reflecting on experience

In insight

Expert groups are more likely to

- Find creative solutions to problems
- Reach ingenious and insightful solutions that do not occur to others

(Continued)

(Continued)

- Distinguish relevant from nonrelevant data when solving problems
- Apply information acquired in other contexts to problem solving

Source: Garmston, 2003

BUILDING SKILLS IN SELF-REFLECTION

Three elements help support self-reflection:

1. *A safe environment.* Group members' sense of safety is better when they know (a) they are not subject to external evaluation; (b) the purpose of their work is self-reflective growth; and (c) they have the power to select their focus for development. In addition, participants own how data are interpreted and used.

2. *A structure.* A map or conversational template that guides participants' interaction helps support their ability to self-reflect. Conversational guides and constraints are useful for groups. Templates must be taught to work groups.

3. *Appropriate tools.* The most important conversational tools supporting self-reflection are those used to encourage thinking. These approaches include not expressing judgment, pausing, paraphrasing, asking open-ended questions, and providing inference-free data.

10

Enhancing Energy Sources

Our traditional school model is based on outdated scientific conceptions of how the world works; schools are operating on a classical basis in a quantum world. Scientific metaphors formulated in the 17th century by Rene Descartes and Isaac Newton depict the universe as a machine and the world as a giant clock. The prevailing view was that the world is made up of tiny, isolated bits of matter that interacted with energy sources (Devall & Sessions, 1985). All of our understandings of the world came from this premise for nearly three centuries—that the world is basically a mechanical system and outside energy acts upon it.

The 20th century brought new understanding through quantum physics that subatomic particles *are* energy, not things. The term *quantum mechanics*—the formal name for this way of studying the world—means bundles of energy (quantum) in motion (mechanics) (Capra, 1991).

In the world of quantum mechanics, elementary matter behaves sometimes as a wave and sometimes as a particle, complementary aspects of a single reality, like the two sides of a coin. As a result, physicists can know the position of the particles or their momentum, but not simultaneously. Quantum matter is influenced by the very act of observation, which connects the observer to the system being observed and influences the system.

The same is true in human systems. In school improvement, we cannot always see what we need to measure, and the act of measuring itself impacts the system. What we measure signals a value judgment which shifts the way time, talent, and money are directed. Basing part of teacher evaluations on student test scores is a problematic example of this phenomenon.

By focusing on the energy that exists at the most basic levels, however, we can move beyond what we register with our five senses. We can attain our goals by studying the flow and interchange of energy—the basic particle of the system—and developing that energy.

As Bruce Wellman and I wrote,

> Before modern times, the precedent existed in the ways we naturally used energy *fields* such as gravity, magnetism, and static electricity. We know of their presence because we have evidence of their results. We can experience their effects, but we cannot hear them. We can feel them, but we cannot see them. We can use them, but we cannot put them in our pocket, or even accurately diagram them.
>
> In the future, we may take for granted that *human* energy fields exist, and that educators can deliberately tend, harvest, and use these fields to help schools and the people within them to be continuously adaptive. (1995, p. 7)

Five such human fields, or states of mind, are *efficacy, flexibility, craftsmanship, consciousness,* and *interdependence* (Costa & Garmston, 2002). High-performing groups find ways to maintain their energy in order to reach high-level goals. The process of continuous self-improvement requires forces that fuel learning and action. These five forces are needed to power through obstacles and effectively resolve conflicts. Group members are only able to absorb new learning and meet new challenges by maintaining high levels of collaborative energy.

Groups build their collaborative energy through work in these five areas. These sources drive, influence, motivate, and inspire the hearts and minds of group members to attain the greatest efficiency in work and highest levels of performance. Taken together, they are forces directing one toward authentic, congruent, ethical behavior, the touchstones of integrity. They are the tools of disciplined choice making which guide human action. We see the effects of the levels of energy in group members' attitudes, language, and actions.

These descriptors for the five energy sources are drawn from Garmston and Wellman's *The Adaptive School* (2009).

EFFICACY

Efficacy is a natural human quest for continuous learning, self-empowerment, mastery, and control. Efficacy transcends race, income level, subject matter, and age. Both individuals and groups can reflect high or low levels of efficacy.

Collective efficacy, the group's belief that members have the capacity to succeed in their efforts and are able and willing to do so, is consistently related to improved student achievement (McLaughlin, 1990; Tschannen-Moran, 2004). Collective efficacy influences group performance by shaping members' behavior and influencing the culture and environment (Goddard, 2001).

Groups with a sense of efficacy believe they have the knowledge, skills, and will to meet their goals and overcome obstacles. As a result, they take actions with this perception in mind. Sense of efficacy is a catalyst for being able to resolve complex challenges. Efficacious groups are creative problem solvers, persevere longer, are more diligent, and achieve their goals. The same is true with individuals—teachers who believe they can successfully reach students help students achieve at higher levels.

Those with low levels of efficacy are characterized by blame, withdrawal, and rigidity. Teachers with a high sense of efficacy have more energy for their work, persevere longer, set more challenging goals, and are more willing to work to overcome obstacles.

Groups with collective efficacy

- Learn from experiences and shape themselves accordingly
- Know what they don't know and what they need to know or do, and develop strategies to meet those needs
- Productively manage the tension between the vision of their desired state and the realities of the existing state
- Focus resources where the resources can make the biggest difference
- Are motivated by and committed to achieving shared goals

FLEXIBILITY

Humans have a unique ability to perceive events from multiple perspectives. We work to change, adapt, and expand our repertoire of responses. Flexibility means setting aside the first answer to delve into other perspectives.

Flexible groups honor different perspectives, are able to shift perspectives, and value diversity. Members see others' perspectives not just to the degree that others' views are the same as theirs. They think rationally—logically, analytically, methodically—and more intuitively—conceptually, discerning themes and patterns from information. Flexible groups use an array of thinking styles and process skills. These groups are able to overcome challenges by generating multiple ideas.

Flexible groups listen with their ears, eyes, hearts, and minds. Group members have high levels of empathy, can foresee misunderstandings, and anticipate ways to avoid them. Both efficacy and flexibility relate to the group's willingness to take calculated risks. Flexible groups generate knowledge and push the envelope on new ways of doing work. They grow continuously.

Flexible groups are able to

- Collectively shift perspectives
- Access a large repertoire of thinking and process skills
- Attend to rational and intuitive ways of working
- Generate and use multiple options for moving past obstacles
- Navigate internal tensions related to confusion and ambiguity
- Honor and make use of diversity within and outside of the group

CRAFTSMANSHIP

Humans yearn to become clearer, more precise, and integrated. Craftsmanship involves setting demanding goals and continuously refining work. Individuals who are craftsmen ceaselessly work to deepen their knowledge, skills, and effectiveness.

Glickman (1991) found that the most successful teachers are the most dissatisfied with their own work. These are people who impose higher standards on themselves and their work. As craftsmanship increases, craftsmen are more self-analytical and evaluative (Garmston & Hyerle, 1988).

Groups that exhibit craftsmanship take pride in their work and are continuously striving to improve. Like musicians, woodworkers, or a host of other highly skilled individuals, educators who are craftsmen drive themselves to learn constantly and to improve their effectiveness at the work they do. They invent new and better ways to accomplish the task. They are standard-setters.

A group that exhibits craftsmanship

- Creates, holds, calibrates, and refines performance and product standards
- Envisions and manages multiple time orientations
- Invests energy in honing and inventing process tools
- Honors the pathway from novice to expert performance
- Continuously refines inter- and intragroup communications

CONSCIOUSNESS

Humans strive to monitor and reflect on their own thoughts and actions. We are aware of our own thoughts, feelings, and behaviors, and our intentions and their effects. Consciousness leads to high energy.

Consciousness means moving beyond habit to making thought-out choices. Groups that are able to act consciously have self-control, self-discipline, and self-direction. Consciousness, however, takes continual reflection and must be practiced regularly. The brain places routine acts into the subconscious in order to maximize efficiency and free the conscious mind. Like becoming aware of old wallpaper that we take for granted, we must act to raise consciousness.

Groups that exhibit this energy keep their values and norms visible. They work to maintain awareness of their identity and purpose, to monitor their beliefs and discrepancies between actual and desired states, and regularly reflect on their processes.

The group with consciousness

- Is aware of how its own assumptions and knowledge interfere with its learning
- Is aware of its core values, norms, and group identity
- Monitors congruence with its meeting standards
- Is explicit and aware of its criteria for decision making
- Is aware of and stands outside itself to reflect on its processes and products

INTERDEPENDENCE

Humans have an innate need for reciprocity, a sense of belonging and connectedness, and desire to join with the larger system and community of which they are a part. Interdependence involves a sense of kinship, unity, and sharing that bonds individuals through shared goals, values, and appreciation for being. According to Sergiovanni

(1994), German sociologist Ferdinand Tonnies called this state *Gemeinschaft*—a community of mental life—in contrast with *Gesellschaft*, in which community values have been replaced with contractual ones. Most organizations are organized around the latter.

Interdependent groups, on the other hand, value and trust multiple relationships. They appreciate and use dialogue and see disagreement not as negative conflict, but as a means to transformative action. They view knowledge as fluid, provisional, and subject to revision based on additional information. Groups with high levels of understanding in this area are aware of how the group relates to other groups and of the interconnectedness of individuals with all levels of systems within the district, community, and planet. These groups see potential where others see walls.

The interdependent group

- Values its interactions and trusts in dialogue
- Is aware of its relationships and how interconnections are sources of mutual influence
- Regards knowledge and knowing as fluid, provisional, and subject to improvement from outside information
- Regards disagreement and conflict as a source of group learning
- Envisions the group's potential

Poole and O'keafor (1989) found that teachers' states of mind predicted how well they would implement a new curriculum. The combination of efficacy and interdependence proved the most significant difference between those who used the curriculum and those who did not. The combination of these two factors made the difference.

PAY ATTENTION TO ENERGY FLOW

Bruce Wellman and I first wrote about Edward Lorenz and self-renewal in *Educational Leadership* (1995). One fated day in

1961, Lorenz, a meteorologist at the Massachusetts Institute of Technology, did something that changed forever our understanding of the use of energy and data in dynamical systems. Lorenz was working on a model for forecasting weather. Discovering that he needed to extend his forecast, he rounded off one number by 0.02% in the computer. He went out for coffee as the computer continued to process the problem while he was out. When he returned, he found a set of numbers that looked nothing like his original forecast.

At that moment, two fresh understandings of the world were born: First, that minor changes in initial conditions will produce major changes in dynamical systems. Lorenz's minute rounding of a number resulted in a significantly different pattern predicted for the weather ahead. Second, more data will not permit more accurate predictions in such systems. Since each event affects another, which in turn affects another, more information complicates forecasting to a point of uncertainty.

Lorenz's work led to the butterfly metaphor popularized in the movie *Jurassic Park*. Because the wind generating from the wings of a butterfly affects tiny air currents around it, and because tiny inputs into dynamical systems create major changes, this theory says a butterfly stirring the air in Beijing can eventually influence a storm system over New York City.

The butterfly principle is at work when fractional changes in degrees of temperature on the ocean surface turn tropical storms into hurricanes. It was also working when, in a middle school, a small group of teachers decided to reverse the norm of negative and putdown humor in the hallways by modeling positive comments to one another and to students. They achieved major changes in this aspect of school culture within three months.

Schools, like weather systems, are nonlinear systems that change radically with the folding and refolding of feedback into themselves. And, since tiny inputs reverberate into big changes, we can work for transformational results by deliberately influencing the right inputs.

Which butterfly wings should schools be blowing on? Since everything influences or potentially influences everything else, the wings to influence are those that are most generative and positive in their effects (Briggs, 1992). The energy fields and the events stimulated by the five states of mind are so webbed in the interactions among people in an organization that the slightest twitch anywhere becomes amplified into unexpected convulsions somewhere else in the system.

Paying attention, then, to the group's energy flow and interchange of energy is important. Consider the information above describing the five energy sources. How would you assess the state of a group of which you are a member? Groups can have members rate the group in the five areas and discuss their thinking. Which areas might be most important to attend to for your group?

Jane Ellison and Carolee Hayes of the Center for Cognitive Coaching have developed a team assessment survey to help groups determine the state of their energy levels. The survey can be purchased through the Cognitive Coaching website at www.cognitivecoaching.com. The survey has 12 questions for each energy source and provides a score that groups can use for item analysis and to set goals. A sample of that self-assessment instrument appears in Appendix B.

These five energy sources influence the group's capacity for gaining knowledge and are related to cognitive, moral, and ego development. The energy sources can be developed in the group and in individuals. Focusing questions on identity, belief, capabilities, behaviors, and environment will keep the group centered on its energy sources both as individual members and as group members. Examples of focusing questions are

1. How did your sense of this being a true professional community guide your interactions today?

2. Reflect for a minute on your beliefs about the importance of collaboration. Keeping your beliefs in mind, what did you notice about the group's work today?

3. In what ways did your understanding of the processes of dialogue and discussion influence your productivity with today's topic?

4. Given the emotional content of today's topic, what were some of the ways that you managed the internal process of the way you listened to one another?

5. What were some of the ways that this seating arrangement supported your work today? Garmston & Wellman, 2009, p. 127)

The five energy sources are individual states of mind that, combined in the group, generate thoughts and actions for group members that help them resolve challenges, overcome personal and group issues, and develop strategies and interventions to create higher levels of learning for both teachers and students. They drive, influence, motivate, and inspire our intellects. These traits form the personality of the group itself.

SECTION IV

Developing Facilitation Skills

11

Developing Facilitation Skills

Schoolwide improvement requires collaborative work toward common goals. Collaborative work sometimes needs facilitation. Groups need skills, structures, and protocols to collaborate effectively. Without these, serious problems arise.

Schools that have formed collaborative learning groups of teachers can benefit from the skills of an experienced facilitator, but an external facilitator is not always available and particularly not for the amount of time it would take to work with each group.

Facilitation is essential for group success. I once was a member of a group of bright, knowledgeable, committed people. We floundered without leadership, each of us, for a time, with good intentions trying to assert leadership within the group. What we needed was one person whose primary concern was about process, and from that vantage point, could provide leadership. While facilitation is important, ultimately group effectiveness is determined more by the collaborative maturity of the group than by a facilitator's knowledge or skill.

For this reason, and to develop teacher leadership, many learning teams are looking within the group for facilitators.

In many settings, teacher leaders can learn facilitation skills to serve groups. Facilitation really is planned improvisation, and a modest repertoire of facilitation strategies and moves can serve a beginning facilitator well in many settings. Among the roles described in Chapter 2 is that of citizen facilitator, a member of a small team who participates in meeting deliberations but also provides facilitation services.

WHAT DOES AN EFFECTIVE FACILITATOR DO?

Facilitators are able to improvise and think on their feet during a meeting because they have spent time preparing and laying the groundwork in areas that can be planned. Good facilitators think about what they need before, during, and after the meeting.

Before the Meeting

The facilitator clarifies the meeting's goals and helps ensure that goals are specific enough for the group to get to its desired outcome. The facilitator ensures that the meeting agenda is clear. The facilitator is responsible for arranging for a meeting place and setting up the room. (See Chapter 15 for room design ideas.) The facilitator arrives as early as possible to check whether the room is ready and supplies are available, as well as to arrange the tables and chairs for efficiency and effectiveness.

Working sessions often require public recording. The facilitator is responsible for arranging for any needed recording materials, such as chart paper, and then for making sure the charts are available and visible to all group members as the meeting progresses.

During the Meeting

The facilitator opens the meeting, clarifies roles, runs an inclusion activity to get all voices and heads in the room, reviews or constructs the agenda with the group, and directs the beginning of the work.

Focus Attention

To begin, the facilitator gets the group's attention. Opening the meeting by speaking before having the group's attention leads to disorganization and needless chaos. Grinder (2007) and Zoller (2010) list specific nonverbal cues that are helpful for gaining immediate attention, many of which are also useful in the classroom. Next, the facilitator may review the role briefly and seek guidance from the group about how firm or soft group members want the facilitation to be.

Clarify the Facilitator's Role

Groups essentially allow themselves to be facilitated. One approach that allows group members to decide the facilitator's role in the group is this: The facilitator draws an imaginary line and organizes points along it using metaphors, naming points from Mr. Rogers to Rambo or from Mary Poppins to Xena, Warrior Princess. Another metaphor might be "lion to lamb." The facilitator then asks the group to point at the region of the line that they would like the facilitation to characterize.

> Presenting choices helps the group to gain or regain the power to control its own direction and purposes. This is especially true if individual group members are dominating the group's time and energies. Such a group will tend to select harder forms of facilitation and give the facilitator permission to intervene with problematic situations. (Lipton, Wellman, & Humbard, 2003, p. 15).

The group's direction gives the facilitator an understanding of how to proceed in the role.

Introduce an Inclusion Activity

Inclusion activities help members transition from activities before the meeting to the meeting itself. In a sense, while people's bodies show up, inclusion activities help the mind to be present as well. These activities also help the group's members move from a state of *me*-ness to a state of *we*-ness, ready to begin collaborative work. Inclusion activities should be brief (they are not the meeting), and give equivalent airtime to each participant.

Some useful inclusion activities are

- *Personal sharing.* Members go around the circle, briefly naming their mood and anything that might detract from their full participation.
- *Check-in.* I learned the "check-in" from teachers in Santa Monica, California. Someone volunteers to go first and indicates she is finished by saying "I'm in," almost like a player might designate his engagement in the play at a poker table.
- *Group groan.* Groups list the best and worst things members think can happen in this session. The facilitator records them on a flip chart. The group agrees that should any of the worst things occur, all will participate in a group groan. Practice the groan once. This lightens up a meeting when needed.

Some additional examples from Wilson High School in the Los Angeles Unified School District:

- *First job.* A middle school faculty and a high school faculty were coming together for their second of three vertical articulation meetings for curriculum cohesion. To build community in a quick and lively way, each participant named, in round-robin fashion, his or her first paying job. After all participants shared, they asked each other a question or two about the commonalities and trends.
- *Modified check-in.* Before a training on sheltered instruction for English language learners (ELL), the trainer modified the check-in activity by presenting these sentence frames on a PowerPoint slide:
  - ☐ "I have been thinking about _____."

☐ "I have been feeling _____, because _____."

☐ "Even though _____ has been on my mind, I'm in. I'm ready to focus on today's ELL session."

Example: "I have been thinking about our new bell schedule. I have been feeling rushed because of the alternating days. Even though the schedule has been on my mind, I'm in. I'm ready to focus on today's ELL session."

After the session, a teacher asked the presenter to go back to the check-in slide so he could photograph it with his phone. He wanted to capture the sentence frames to use with his students before they began the day's lesson!

Of special note in inclusion activities is that group members should honor the activity and not engage in side talk. After everyone has spoken, the facilitator may create a summary paraphrase of what group members have said.

Frame the Work

Part of the facilitator's job is setting a tone for the meeting by describing the purpose of the work and how the group will benefit. The purpose should be broad enough to allow members to relate to the spirit of the work without getting too fixated on details. Specifics can come later. Outcomes might be described using verbs such as *decide, recommend, inform, assess, explore, advocate, inquire,* or *identify*.

These introductory activities take longer to explain than to do. All of these introductory elements can be combined and blended so as not to take much time. The facilitator now has helped get the meeting underway. What next?

Keep an Eye on the Goals

During the meeting, the facilitator keeps the agenda in mind more closely than group members do, so is responsible for helping the group remain on task. Experienced facilitators become skilled at monitoring the group's energy, using strategies to pace the meeting and redirect attention, and activating members' relevant knowledge. Eliciting members' prior knowledge can help level the playing field within the group. The facilitator may ask members to recall and summarize actions taken at the last meeting, ask the group to respond individually to a prompt and then to sort the responses, or use other strategies that maintain a safe learning space.

The facilitator gives directions according to activities on the agenda, leads processes, and offer guidelines and suggestions. The facilitator helps the group transition from one segment of the meeting to another, helping members shift without losing their momentum. The facilitator announces or has the group summarize the conclusion reached in the meeting. Classroom teachers will have strategies in mind from their teaching experience to accomplish these aspects of the work and can practice modifying the strategies for adults.

Closing the Meeting

Properly closing the meeting will help the group feel more satisfied with what members have accomplished. The facilitator ensures that several tasks are completed to successfully wrap up the session.

Task Assignment

The facilitator makes sure that actionable items are clearly spelled out and the group knows who will do what by when. When members don't review these matters, the result can be confusion and low morale when work is not completed. The information should be recorded in the group's minutes or on a wall chart.

Commitment Test

Some group members may have a tendency to overcommit and find themselves struggling later to complete their assigned tasks. By raising realities and articulating potential conflicts, the facilitator helps the group explore ways to overcome any barriers. In one form of a commitment test, the facilitator says,

"I know none of you would deliberately sabotage the agreements you've made, but if you were to do that, what would drive you to do so?"

Communication

In every organization, when something goes wrong, staff members inevitably blame the problem on "communication." In the frenetic pace of schools today, attention to communication is even more essential. A meeting summary distributed no more than a day after the meeting signals the importance of the group's work. The facilitator may even stay immediately after the meeting, with help, to complete this task. Other communication may involve e-mailing information to the principal or other departments or learning teams, posting minutes in the staff room, or designating group members to verbally communicate results or actions to specified colleagues.

Assessment

I can't stress this point enough: Any group too busy to reflect on its work is too busy to improve. A few minutes at the end of the meeting to complete an assessment is an opportunity for professional learning for the whole group. The group may develop a survey to determine how effective the group was, how well members followed meeting norms, or to consider other factors of the group's work. A team member can compile the data and present the results at the next meeting, noting the frequency distribution for each item. Groups should begin a meeting by discussing the assessment results and noting what members need to do in order to improve the group's effectiveness. The self-monitoring Meeting Inventory in Chapter 9 is one tool groups may use or may use as a basis for customizing their own.

Arranging for the Next Meeting

If the facilitator is a rotating role, the group may specify who will take the job at the next meeting. Group members may also suggest agenda items or arrange for how the agenda will be created for the next meeting.

FIVE QUALITIES OF A GOOD FACILITATOR

Good facilitators pay attention to developing five specific personal qualities. They are

Clarity

Effective facilitators use precise language to help the group avoid frustration and to eliminate ambiguity. They model for group members a human goal of being organized, brief, and specific with their words. Clarity involves

- Using words and phrases that have a single meaning.
- Avoiding pronouns, especially *they* and *I*.
- Helping the group relate members' work to the big picture.
- Using organizing language to outline the work, such as saying, "The process involves three steps. The first step is . . . ."

Facilitators also are absolutely clear when they shift to the role of group participant. They signal a role change by asking someone else to take the facilitator's space for a while, or by moving to a different part of the room and asking, "May I take off my facilitator hat for a while to make a comment?" Once the facilitator is done with the group member role, he or she goes back to the original facilitation spot (without speaking en route) as the meeting moves forward. Physically moving to the new space helps observers psychologically separate the individual's two roles. People believe what their eyes tell them more than what their ears hear.

Consciousness

Good facilitators strive to be aware of what is happening around them, but at the same time to be aware of their internal world. They look for body language cues from other group members, listen for voice nuances, and stay focused. They are aware of the environment—room temperature and conditions, and whether everyone can see. They notice when they are becoming fatigued themselves, their own assumptions or points of view, and their relationship to the group. They fine-tune their external and internal awareness so each complements the other. Good facilitators understand that the group benefits when the facilitator gains new understanding that can help guide the group to different interactions and help members see matters in a different light.

Competence

Practice, experience, and especially reflection help develop the quality of competence. Competent facilitators work to understand ways to develop productive practices and the essentials of effective meetings. They understand how to use discussion and when dialogue is more beneficial. They study theories of adult learning and nonverbal language and work on their skills in language and intervening. They recognize that the best-laid plans may need to be altered, and they are wise enough to see when a plan is not working.

Confidence

One's sense of efficacy translates into actions that end in results. The belief that we have the knowledge and skills to facilitate a group drives attention and effort that can help overcome many obstacles. Every person brings a unique blend of skills and talents to the role, as well as needed skills. Experience, reflection, support, and mentoring help to develop the facilitator's confidence.

Credibility

The facilitator is not granted credibility immediately but develops it through interaction with the group. Credibility may be defined as the group's belief that the facilitator is competent, confident, neutral, trustworthy, and fair. Facilitators lose credibility when they are less than forthcoming, don't admit their mistakes, or disrespect others. Getting past a mistake may take acknowledging the error in a statement, apologizing for it, and perhaps using some self-deprecating humor. Resolving missteps in this manner helps the group regain focus and direction.

GROWING AS A FACILITATOR

Just as most teachers start out with few classroom management skills and develop them with time, patience, and practice, so facilitators mature over time. Principals, staff developers, and teacher leaders read, research about the best practices for leading meetings, and spend time practicing facilitation skills.

Some essential facilitation skills, including paraphrasing, pausing, probing, and inquiring, can be practiced in almost any everyday situation. Practicing these skills will help them to become an unconscious part of the facilitator's repertoire so the facilitator is better able to focus on the meeting and external issues. Expert facilitators have internalized the skills and can integrate them in chunks without thinking, freeing up their conscious mind to attend to the dynamics of the meeting. Paraphrasing cannot be practiced too much. Most of these skills can be practiced in the classroom, also.

GROW YOUR CONFIDENCE

Some tips for growing in confidence include:

- Listen to a conversation without looking at the speakers. Record what you hear. Or watch the group and try to get a sense of members' energy levels. Monitor members' breathing to learn to sense and anticipate the group's mood.

- Pay attention to your body language. Monitor how you stand, your breathing in different situations, your tone of voice, the rhythm of your language, your heart rate. Be aware of when your muscles tense, changing your body signals. Try changing your posture to create a different set of nonverbal cues. The warriors with Genghis Khan were effective because of their sensory acuity. They only released their arrows when all four of the horse's feet were in the air.
- Hold something in your hand when facilitating, such as a pencil. Many people find having something to hold is a way to feel more grounded.
- Keep your focus on the group rather than yourself.
- Grow your repertoire. Watch skilled leaders and note their language, then copy what you think makes them successful. Practice phrases first with your students. Make notes of phrases you want to use during group facilitation.
- Facilitate vicariously. Ask experts why they took certain actions and for ideas, suggestions, and support.

Within learning communities, group members examine student work, talk about data, plan, look for solutions to problems, and reflect on their own learning. Facilitators guide the group using planned agendas and selected protocols. Yet the unexpected can and frequently does happen. Facilitation, like teaching, is cognitively complex. In addition, the facilitator has the added tension of practicing new leadership skills in front of colleagues.

Relationships, emotions, perceptions, and decisions inform facilitator behaviors. Because of this, potential facilitators must recognize the mental agility required in facilitation work. Effective facilitators use metacognitive processes that answer the question, "How will I use the skills and knowledge that I have?"

They develop mental aptitudes focused on

1. Identifying their intentions and choosing congruent behaviors

2. Setting aside unproductive patterns of listening and responding

3. Knowing when to intervene

4. Supporting the group's purposes, topics, processes, and development

The next several chapters will explore the most critical aspects of these aptitudes in greater depth.

The role of facilitator may be one that few teachers have attempted or mastered. Yet facilitation is essential to developing effective groups. For teachers, the facilitator's role offers an opportunity to lead without leaving the classroom. As teachers increasingly take on more responsibilities, working within a mature, supportive, collaborative group to develop new skills and abilities can refresh and renew the adult learner.

12

Learning the Language of Facilitation

The facilitator's main task is to help the group increase effectiveness by improving its process and structure. *Process* refers to how a group works together. It includes how members talk to each other, how they identify and solve problems, how they make decisions, and how they handle conflict. *Structure* refers to stable, recurring group process, for example group membership or group roles. In contrast, *content* refers to what a group is working on (Schwarz, 2002, p. 5).

When groups plan, solve problems, share information, evaluate, and make decisions, their work is immeasurably enhanced by an effective facilitator. The facilitator is the group's instrument for expressing and understanding relevant ideas and information.

KNOW YOUR INTENTIONS

Facilitators work to sustain the group's spirit of inquiry and protect the group from identifying and accepting the easiest—but not necessarily the best—solution. The facilitator helps group members focus, engage, and connect. Being clear about the intention of an action will help the facilitator with decision making. Knowing one's intention is the source of impulse control, patience, strategic listening, and strategic speaking. Intention keeps the facilitator from reactive rather than proactive behavior.

The facilitator stays acutely aware of any signs of distress in the group, such as group members expressing frustration with the process or members asking clumsy and off-putting questions. The facilitator works hard to search for language and strategies that will guide the group back to active inquiry.

Having clear intentions is a special facilitation attribute. New facilitators can improve their skill in clarifying intentions by rehearsing in calm situations. When preparing for a conversation with a parent, ask, *What is my intention?* When observing a colleague's classroom, again ask, *What is my intention?* Attend a social event—*What is my intention?* Exercising this mental ability when the heat is low makes it accessible when temperatures rise.

SET ASIDE UNPRODUCTIVE LISTENING

Effective facilitators set aside unproductive forms of listening, and they help groups develop by helping members become aware of these meeting time-wasters. The facilitator might introduce these ideas to a group with a text as expert strategy using "Four mental aptitudes help facilitators facing challenges," from the winter 2008 *Journal of Staff Development* (Garmston, 2008a).

Unproductive listening involves

- Solution listening—thinking of or listening for a solution while the speaker is still talking. The thought bubble may include this: "I know what to do."
- Autobiographical listening—mentally focusing on a personal experience related to what is being described. The thought bubble might include: "Me too!"

- Inquisitive listening—asking for details unrelated to conversation's goal. The thought bubble might be: "Tell me more."

While these are all normal forms of listening and sometimes are useful, they interfere with a facilitator's ability to attend to others' communication.

Solution Listening

Seeking solutions is normal. Humans are wired to look for patterns and seek to create meaning. In addition, status, rewards, and identity all are tied up with being a good problem solver.

The solution frame is deeply embedded in educators' psyches. Time pressures in schools push people toward action and away from reflection. Solution listening, however, is not productive and violates facilitator neutrality, the core principle in facilitation. Most importantly, the listener cannot deeply understand what the other is trying to communicate if he or she is forming a solution and rehearsing a response.

Autobiographical Listening

When group members practice autobiographical listening, it can lead to endless story telling, which has little value to a group. This is dinner party conversation, not productive meeting talk. In addition, listeners in this mode are filtering information as they try to hear another's story through the lens of their own experiences. While it might be a source of empathy, an autobiographical frame can lead to distortion and miscommunication. When facilitators attend to their own autobiographical listening, they interfere with their ability to understand perspectives of group members.

Inquisitive Listening

The inquisitive frame is sometimes triggered by the autobiographical. People inquire to see how others' stories compare to their own. Pure curiosity also motivates inquisitive listening, responding, and inquiring. But not all details have equal importance. Facilitators help themselves and group members distinguish those details worthy of attention and those that are just interesting.

Learn to Question

A good question is probably the second most important language strategy a facilitator can use. The first is the paraphrase, which communicates, among other things, "I am trying to understand you." We received improper training in the 1960s regarding paraphrasing when it was thought that paraphrasing was a language skill. "I think I hear you saying" is off-putting to many because it sounds formulaic and it's about what the listener is doing with the message, not about the message. The proper pronoun is *you*: "So, you are wondering/considering/ feeling/examining . . . . ." See Chapter 6, which discusses paraphrasing as one of the seven norms.

Because a paraphrase elicits more information, it can be used to inquire, sometimes less intrusively than a well-constructed question. When we paraphrase, we operate within the other person's map. When we question, the map we operate from is our own, and even the best question might be taken as a little bit intrusive.

What makes questioning tricky is that humans are quick to perceive threats. Messages—what we see, the tone of what we hear, the words of a question—send messages to the brain's emotional center before the message can reach the cognitive processing center. The amygdala is responsible for detecting threats—and it is *fast*. If we perceive threat, blood floods the brain stem, and we are incapable of cognitive processing. We move instead to flight, fight, or freeze, valuable positions when faced with physical danger, but counterproductive in group interactions.

A question that supports inquiry—our most important function as professionals collaborating with each other—is constructed to be invitational. An invitational question has three parts. First, it is asked with an approachable voice, a voice pattern with a melodic lilt, usually at the end of sentences curling up. In Kendall Zoller's research (2010) on classroom management techniques, he noticed that in all languages he studied, effective teachers asked questions with an approachable voice and gave directions in a credible voice—one in which the tonal pattern is flatter and tends to curl down at the end of sentences. A second quality of an invitational question is that it uses plurals. Instead of asking, "What idea do you have?" the more invitational form is, "What *ideas* do you have?" Third, invitational questions use tentative or exploratory language like *some* ideas, *possible* ideas, *might* instead of *may*, and *a* instead of *the*.

Questions can help us see our work from different angles, better understand the details of a situation, make better decisions, be more flexible in our views, and get better results. Questions engage us, enhance our thinking, and develop our intellects. Questions that cause people to think lead to greater learning than statements do. Increased information makes available more choices. More choices yield better decisions. And better teacher decisions ultimately benefit not only the group, but students in the classroom as well.

Educators have a rich history of questioning, beginning with Socrates. Yet most teachers know how difficult it is to construct a good question. Where a question is focused determines its mediative power.

Questions directed at internal resources enhance self-directed learning. These questions ask about the group member's knowledge, skills, attitudes, or states of mind needed to accomplish a task or solve a problem: "Who do you need to be in order to do that?" "What skills will you use to accomplish that?" or "How will you know what is the best decision?"

Questions directed internally at a desired state invite goal-oriented thinking. Examples are "How do you want them to feel?" or "How will you know you are satisfied?"

Questions directed to external goals also invite goal-oriented thinking and provide information from which planning can result. Examples are: "What do you want to accomplish?" and "What might you see or hear when they have learned it?"

Questions directed at an existing state gather data, but they have no mediative power. For example, asking, "What have you already tried?" yields information, but does not further the group's ability to work toward a goal.

ANATOMY OF A MEDIATIVE QUESTION

Some questions are more powerful than others. We say these questions have *mediative* properties. Mediative questions

- Are open-ended, allowing many possible answers. Using the plural form facilitates this intention—goals instead of goal, causes instead of cause
- Convey positive presuppositions about the respondent. For example, you might say, "As an experienced teacher . . . what might you . . . ?"
- Are judgment-free
- Use exploratory language: "How might you . . . " or "What are some possible ways . . . "
- Signal inquiry through the facilitator's use of the approachable voice
- Invite thinking to one of three levels: knowledge, comprehension-analysis-synthesis, or application-evaluation. Costa (1985) called these input, process and output
- Link to the respondent's state of mind and cognitive style
- Cross categories: "As you consider alternatives, what seems most promising?"

You can help others refine their questioning skills by using two supports, *scaffolding* and a *word bank*.

Scaffolding

Scaffolding helps facilitators formulate effective questions. Repetition will help make this template automatic for facilitators to be able to compose a variety of questions. With repetition, anyone can achieve range and automaticity.

A Scaffold for Questioning

Question Stems	Cognitive Processes	Focus
As you . . .	Recall	Internal
What are some of . . .	Compare	Your reaction
How might you . . .	Predict	Your feelings
How did you . . .	Infer	Your values
What led to . . .	Know	Your assumptions
What possible . . .	Analyze	External
What might . . .	Envision	His behavior
		That interaction
		That event
		That lesson
		That meeting
		That committee
Question stems in column 1, delivered as invitations to question, signal the mind that a friendly question is coming.	The second column asks the respondent to perform a specific cognitive function.	The third column represents some possible focuses for the question, either toward the participant's internal experience or toward external stimuli.

Practice composing questions by combining a word or phrase from each of the three columns. Experiment with different sequences.

Using a Word Bank

Diane Zimmerman (1995) directed our attention to asking *cross-categorical* questions. These questions invite the framer to consider multiple categories (*what, when, how, why*) in the same question. "*How* will you know *when . . . ?*" Developing a collection of personal word banks aids the staff developer in having a ready-at-hand vocabulary with which to compose questions. A word bank can be a list of verbs naming cognitive processes or synonyms for conceptual areas that might be the focus of mediative questioning. (See Figure 12.1.)

Let's say you wish to ask a question that will cause listeners to reflect on their beliefs and values. Choose any verb from the list below to invite a specific cognitive process. Now select one or more of the words under beliefs or values, and design a question using both.

Here are some examples:

"How might you *decide* the *worth* of that activity?"

"As you *assess* the *importance* of that strategy, what *theories* are guiding you?"

"Which *assumptions* seem to have the greatest *merit?*"

USE THE LANGUAGE OF FACILITATION

Learning to facilitate groups takes practice. One way to learn is to isolate, analyze, and practice skill subsets. Use the list below

Figure 12.1   Word Bank for Beliefs and Values

Verbs	Beliefs and Values	
assess	view	worth
appraise	sentiment	merit
evaluate	opinion	usefulness
estimate	persuasion	premise
decide	position	benefits
appreciate	judgment	assumptions
admire	conclusion	importance
know	inference	consequence
connect	theory	significance

and add phrases you might use for each category. Compare the language you typically use with the examples, and decide which are most useful. The examples are not "best" phrases and are not the only ones to help achieve positive outcomes. Language will vary depending on the facilitator's style and the group context, but these ideas are a starting place.

COMMON FACILITATION PURPOSES

FOCUS

1. Get attention.

2. Clarify purpose.

3. Give directions.

ENGAGE

4. Enlist participation.

5. Enlarge perspectives.

6. Invite group awareness.

CONNECT

7. Foster understanding.

8. Promote agreements.

To Focus the Group

Be organized. Be brief. Be specific. Use words and phrases that have only one meaning. Introduce the task to the group, clarify ways the task and goal relate to a larger purpose or context for the work and the outcomes members have agreed to for each stage.

Sample language to use for

Getting Attention

- Please stop and look in this direction.
- Let's push the pause button.
- Can everyone hear what Rita is saying?

Clarifying Purpose

- Today's task is to _____ (approve, generate, select, identify, explore, resolve).
- We have three issues: What happened in the past, what we can do now, and what we can do in the future. Our focus today is what we can do now.
- Today we need to (name task). During this meeting, we will (specify tasks).

Giving Directions

- At the last meeting, you analyzed data. Now the task is to look for causal factors. The first step is to . . . .
- Let's identify some ideas to explore. Think of your two most important ideas and prepare to share.
- Work with a partner and identify your most urgent concerns about the project.
- This is a three-step process. First, you will _____, then you will _____, and finally _____.

For the greatest effect, post the directions on charts or on slides. Posting has two advantages. One is that the information stays visible while the group works on the task. Another benefit is that when the group can see the directions, the facilitator can simply point to them as the next task. When directions have two steps or more, put them on a chart or slide.

To Engage the Group

In the following phrases, the language moves from prescriptive statements toward more interpretative comments.

Facilitators use descriptive rather than evaluative words. It's important to assume that each group member has a valuable contribution and will share if he or she feels psychologically safe. Using partners for sharing can help create psychological safety. Give people choices to empower them. Use proper nouns rather than pronouns. Help the group examine an issue from an outside perspective by providing scaffolds.

To Enlist Participation

Some things a facilitator might say are

- I have some suggestions for getting the most value from today's meeting. If someone says something you don't understand, ask for clarification. If an idea is too abstract and you need a concrete example, please ask for it.
- If you disagree with an idea, let the group know. Use the phrase, "I see this differently."
- Everyone in our group may have a comment about this task. Let's give each person a turn. Terrell, you're first; Sally will be second. Juan will follow, and then Tiara. Remember your order. OK, Terrell, please start us off.
- What concerns do you have about this issue?
- Can we hear from someone who hasn't spoken?

A WORD ABOUT PRONOUNS

When you are facilitating a group and are not a member of the group, use the pronoun *you*. When you are a member of a group that you are facilitating, use the inclusive pronoun *we*.

To Enlarge Perspectives

- What patterns, categories, or themes do you see in these data?

- The group has identified what you will see when students are succeeding. What will you hear?
- What inferences, explanations, or conclusions might you draw?
- To begin, you will brainstorm questions about this initiative.

To Invite Group Awareness

- What's going on right now?
- What does the group want to do?
- The group seems to be stuck. Is there something important that's not being talked about?
- The initial conversation was about assessment. The last few comments have been about schedules. Where do you want to focus?
- People seem tired. Do you want to take a break or push on for another 15 minutes?
- How is the group doing on your norm of listening to one another? Talk to a partner.

To Connect With the Group

A facilitator might use these examples for

Fostering understanding:

- Danesh, could you paraphrase what Diane said? Diane, did he get it right? (If not . . .) Diane, say it again.
- Can you specify what you mean by the word *accelerate*?
- Geraldo seems to be advocating doing this immediately, and Robert is recommending more time. Can someone give additional reasons for each position?
- Francis, I think Eduardo is saying he wants to increase requirements for all students, not just the middle students. Is that right, Eduardo? Eduardo, do you understand what Francis is saying?

- I think the group is clear about what you want to do, Aldo. What they are asking for is why. Can you help the group understand the reasons?

Promoting agreements:

- Are you ready to decide?
- What values will drive the decision-making process?
- OK, what different ideas have you heard? What solution might accommodate all of them?
- Two positions seem to have been expressed. Can we have one person representing each position agree to meet separately and bring a recommendation back to the whole group?
- I think I hear everyone agreeing on that point. Can we do a quick check? Thumbs up, you agree. Down, you disagree. Sideways, you're not sure or don't care.

   Take stock of the signal and follow up with those who oppose the majority view. Try a question like
  - ☐ Can you explain your concerns? What would need to be different for you to feel OK about this decision?
  - ☐ Is your opinion a matter of preference or principle?
  - ☐ Are you willing to give it a try until the next reporting period?
- Write your understandings of the group's decision. Share it with the person next to you and edit it if necessary.

   (The group should listen to some of the statements and edit, if needed, as a group.)

BUILD YOUR REPERTOIRE

Pay attention to others' facilitation styles and language. Jot down phrases they use. Isolate language from one or two of the purposes above to practice. Jot down in advance phrases you would like to incorporate into your next facilitation. Practice facilitation phrases when working with students. Keep in mind that knowing is different from understanding. To understand, groups must explain, apply, or interpret information. Have these types of thinking be a focus for your facilitation outcomes.

The Facilitator's Emotional Intelligence

Events trigger facilitators' feelings. Perhaps you experience satisfaction from witnessing a group using a conflict tool you've taught, such as saying *and* instead of *but*. Or perhaps you feel confused and uncertain when events seem to spin out of control. Perhaps you are frustrated when the group abandons the planned agenda. Or perhaps you are embarrassed because your facilitation is not living up to your standards.

These feelings are normal when facilitating. Both the most and the least experienced facilitators experience these and other emotions. What distinguishes the superior facilitator is being able to manage these feelings. Significant writing has been done on what we call emotional intelligence (Goleman, 1995.) Emotional intelligence is the ability to identify, assess, and manage the emotions of oneself, others, or groups. Powell's study of teachers' emotional intelligence (Powell, 2010) finds that teachers who have strong emotional intelligence support more effective and efficient student learning than those with limited emotional intelligence. The study offers considerable evidence to support this contention, including evidence that emotional intelligence is malleable and can be developed. In other words, teachers, even gifted ones, can raise their emotional intelligence. It seems reasonable to assume this is also true of facilitators.

Emotional intelligence is, in part, recognizing and learning to manage one's physiological tendencies related to stress. When facilitators feel threatened in a meeting because they are losing control or rapport with a group, the cortisol and adrenaline flood the brain. The neocortex shuts down, and decision making is hampered. Common reactions are flight, fight, or freeze, although new research finds the flight, fight, or freeze syndrome is more common in males than females. Psychologist Shelley Taylor suggests that the female stress physiology can be quite different. She argues that in most species, females are less aggressive than males and that females, as primary caregivers for offspring, do not resort to the flight option. Taylor suggests that the female stress response is closer to "tend and befriend," that under stress, females revert to an unconscious identity as friend in which a relationship is presupposed and a primary goal is to protect the relationship (Taylor et al., 2000).

The brain, at a scant 56 ounces, consumes up to 30% of the body's oxygen. When we experience stress, our breathing becomes shallow, and we might actually hold our breath. The neocortex, the site of reasoning and language, on the other hand, requires a full supply of oxygen in order to function.

Some ideas to manage neurophysiology are

- Adopt a body posture of calmness and centeredness. Faking it leads to making it and affects your entire system.
- Take two deep breaths to restore oxygen to your brain.
- Release tension in your shoulders.
- Move to another part of the room while breathing deeply.
- Recognize and label feelings as you have them. Naming feelings activates the prefrontal cortex and reduces activity in the limbic system (Rock, 2009), allowing you to have emotions and not be affected by them.
- Paraphrase to diffuse your own and others' emotional tension.
- Ask yourself, "What is the most generous interpretation of an individual's or the group's behavior?"
- Instruct members to talk among themselves on a topic pertinent to the conversation to allow yourself to recover.

In addition, maintain your emotional balance by reminding yourself:

1. People (even you) are rarely as benevolent as they perceive themselves to be.

2. Others are rarely as evil as their opponents perceive them to be.

3. People rarely spend as much time thinking about the issues as is assumed.

4. People rarely plan or think out their behavior. Most aspects of conflict spin off other events and are not the result of cold-hearted calculation.

5. Almost all behaviors are motivated by positive intentions. These intentions frequently arise from people trying to take care of and protect themselves.

6. Previous patterns taint present perceptions. Every conflict has a history that extends beyond the present.

7. Go to the balcony and observe the interactions within the group whenever you have difficulty remembering any of the above.

13

Intervening Successfully

In-ter-ven-tion: *An action taken in order to change what is happening or might happen in order to prevent something undesirable or improve group performance.*

"Who do you think *you* are?"

The group's facilitator could read the reaction on the faces of her colleagues. As a team member, this woman was not a hired or highly experienced facilitator. But the group had committed to rotating the facilitator role every few months to allow those who wanted to develop leadership skills to gain facilitation experience. It happened that this facilitator's turn came as the group was beginning to make several crucial decisions about key aspects of its work. I was visiting the school and was observing the team, no doubt adding to the facilitator's discomfort.

Facilitation is hard work. Learning when to intervene and when to step back may be one of the biggest challenges the facilitator faces. This group had the right idea; a mature group allows facilitation. What this facilitator needed, however, was a way to respond immediately and a way to determine in future how to intervene.

The group's facilitator in this case felt her confidence drain away in the face of her colleagues' reaction. Her nervous system automatically flooded her body with stress hormones. Her heart raced, and her breathing was faster.

What she needed was to direct blood back to her neocortex, the center of reason. Four moves accomplish this: pausing, taking a breath, moving to a new space, and paraphrasing. By letting her colleagues know that she recognized their emotions and understood them, she could honor their feelings. Good facilitators can evoke a useful conversation even in the face of counterproductive behavior.

THE FACILITATOR'S ROLE

To *facilitate* means "to make easier." A facilitator serves the group by working to help group members make easier or more effective their dialogue, decision making, planning, or problem solving. The facilitator's role is to support group members as they share information and ideas. Facilitators remain neutral and do not participate in the group except in cases in which they are a working member of a small group and acting as a citizen facilitator (see Chapter 2 for a definition).

Group members grant the facilitator permission to intervene and redirect group energy and group processes. Facilitators also can make a contract with the group at the outset, giving the facilitator permission to intervene. Facilitators intervene when they direct procedures, choreograph energy within the group, or help the group maintain focus. They intervene to redirect individuals or counterproductive group patterns that detract from the group's ability to get work done. The group's effectiveness can be diminished by

- Unfounded satisfaction with the status quo, because dissatisfaction leads groups to seek refinements;
- Waning efficacy, as members get bogged down and lose confidence that their work can produce results; or
- An absence of effective collaboration around common goals.

Unfounded Satisfaction

In many groups, especially collaborative teams, a primary unspoken or underlying goal is to not rock the boat but to get along with one another, typically in close working relationships. In these groups, members often come to agreement too quickly. Humans are uncomfortable with unresolved issues and want quick answers or solutions. Research on group decision making shows that groups are attracted to the first viable solution they find. As mentioned in the Preface, Herbert Simon, a Nobel laureate in economics, coined the term *satisficient* to express groups' tendencies to settle for what is minimally satisfying and sufficient. Facilitators must work to have groups avoid solutions that are merely satisficient and find the best possible solution.

Waning Efficacy

Teams also face the possibility of getting bogged down. Group members may feel defensive or become adversarial when someone expresses a new idea or introduces new data. Another human tendency is to advocate one's own position without closely examining others' points; another is to resist careful examination of our own orientation. We often do not even realize how our opinion is formed. Group members in these situations may begin to question others' intentions and ascribe to them a negative motive. Chapter 7 explored affective conflict; that is, emotional and intrapersonal conflict, of which diminished group effectiveness is the consequence. Cognitive conflict—disagreement about ideas—leads to sound discourse and problem solving.

Absence of Effective Collaboration

Finally, a very common danger in groups is the absence of common goals. This confusion often stems from a lack of clarity about the group's decision-making authority. Without clarity, group members typically assume they have more decision-making authority than they do, so members feel they have had only token involvement if decisions later are made at the top. When groups are dissatisfied with the results of work to which they contributed, they are dissatisfied with the process.

FACILITATORS CAN ASSIST

Facilitators interrupt and redirect the group when they sense that intervention will prevent the decline of the internal resources of efficacy, craftsmanship, flexibility, consciousness, and interdependence.

Anticipate Issues

Effective facilitators anticipate issues and prepare to help the group maintain collaboration. The facilitator reminds the group of agreed-on norms and processes. The facilitator might say, "You know, teams tend to settle for the first viable idea. Why don't we keep going until we have at least three ideas on the table?" The facilitator clarifies the group's role in decision-making and checks for participants' understanding before moving ahead.

Provide Protocols

To avoid defensiveness or members assigning negative intentions to others, facilitators provide protocols for topics that are hard to talk about. Protocols inform the type of thinking members will do, draw boundaries around conversations, and offer psychological safety. For example, brainstorming helps generate ideas. Round-robin talk allows time for each person to speak. Paraphrase Passport, in which each new speaker must paraphrase the preceding speaker as a "passport" before speaking, is a protocol designed to assist listening (Garmston & Wellman, 2009).

Explain Processes

One of the most effective yet simple ideas is to explain to participants why a particular process will be helpful. Explaining the reason for a particular protocol inevitably reduces group members' resistance and focuses members on what is most relevant—the content or purpose for the group's work.

Build Understanding

Teams need collective understanding of an issue to be able to work on improving student learning. To build collective understanding, facilitators help group members see relationships among systems and also to identify systems. To understand systems relationships, the group needs the cognitive and emotional skills of inquiry, curiosity, and the discipline to ask, "What factors are contributing to this problem?"

Follow Meeting Standards

When members know and practice the five meeting standards (one topic at a time, one process at a time, balanced participation, safe engagement in cognitive conflict, and understanding meeting roles), meetings are more efficient and effective. Facilitators help groups remember and follow the standards.

Develop Skills to Talk Together

Teams must learn how to talk together. Members need to learn fundamental communication skills such as getting ideas heard, paraphrasing, pausing, and balancing inquiry and advocacy (Garmston & Wellman, 1998) as well as the difference between dialogue—talking to understand—and discussion—talking to decide (see Chapter 6 of this book). Facilitators help colleagues as the group learns these skills by helping the group assess its effectiveness and target future improvement.

Generate Compelling Conversations

Good facilitators work to help the group achieve a spirit of inquiry and conscious curiosity. Facilitators might use visual dialogue displays (see box) to spark conversations about difficult topics. A visual dialogue display is a cognitive organizer and a visual prompt to help people think. It helps clarify the boundaries of the conversation and the selected form of thinking, and promotes psychological safety so people are free to contribute (Garmston & Wellman, 1998).

VISUAL DIALOGUE DISPLAYS

Visual dialogue displays are constructed on flip charts or wall charts. They keep the focus on one topic and one process at a time. One example is a force field analysis. In one column, a group records all the forces that would help an innovation succeed. In the second column, members record the forces working against success. They study each column, select the most powerful forces in each, and discuss ways they can strengthen the forces for success while decreasing the forces against.

An extraordinary educator and staff developer, Suzanne Bailey, introduced me to visual dialogue displays and the *domain map*. This map is helpful in the early stages of addressing a challenge. To use a domain map, draw a small box in the center of a flip chart page. Pose a question in the center of the box: "What are the main

features and characteristics of the problem?" All potential answers are written above lines that emanate from
sides of the box.

Sometimes a domain map will evolve into second-
and third-order domain maps as members elaborate on
one of the answers offered in the first domain map. In
other words, if X were one of the answers on the first
domain map, a second map would address, "What are
the main features and characteristics of X?"

DECIDING TO INTERVENE

The difference between good and extraordinary facilitation lies
in the facilitator's decision-making and repertoire. The more
extensive the repertoire of intervention strategies, the more
effective the corrections—but knowing strategies is insufficient.
Before using any strategy, you must be emotionally grounded
and cognitively prepared.

Being grounded allows you to be aware of the whole room,
and to view events and patterns while considering ways to
monitor and adjust behaviors. Various strategies can be used to
ground yourself.

To help stay grounded, plan processes to use with each
agenda topic. Should brainstorming be used with one agenda
item, for example? What decision-making process will the
group follow once ideas have been explored?

Another way to remain grounded is to be crystal clear
about the meeting's goals and each agenda topic. Review these
for yourself and be sure the group understands them before
working on an agenda item. Be able to state each in a simple
declarative statement. Know what the group will see and hear
when each goal is met. Have a conversation at the beginning
of new topics to check for understanding and get the group
aligned on goals and processes at the beginning of an agenda
item. Doing so reduces the need for facilitation as the conversation continues.

Intervention requires careful consideration. Roger Schwarz (2002) has a list of questions to help decide when to intervene. I have found these invaluable in my work. The five most crucial considerations:

1. Is it important?
2. Am I the best person to intervene?
3. Are my observations accurate?
4. Will it be quick or take time?
5. Can the group learn from it?

Is Intervening Important?

Is the behavior significantly disruptive? Groups are fueled by intellectual and emotional energy, a common focus and process, transparent decision making, and fully disclosed information. Group members' participation and consciousness about group work are components of this fuel.

Before intervening and affecting the group's energy, analyze immediate and long-term effects. Consider whether the behavior is disruptive enough to hamper the group's work, how much the work is being hampered (is it delayed, slowed, or completely thrown off track), and whether the behavior will lead to other behaviors that will result in decreased productivity as time goes on. Side talk, for example, can often be ignored if it is not affecting the rest of the group's attentiveness.

Also consider the group's development. Can the group learn from the moment and become more aware of members' behaviors and choices, adding to the group's ability to self-monitor and self-correct?

Am I the Best Person to Intervene?

Sometimes a message from fellow group members can be more potent than a message from the facilitator. For example, in one group, a single member dominated airtime. Three colleagues became extremely annoyed and asked the facilitator to point out the behavior. In this case, the facilitator *could* take on the task of delivering the message, but it would be much more powerful coming from the three irritated members who owned the problem.

Are My Observations Accurate?

Our own observations and interpretations can be wrong. Our perceptions are not trustworthy when we are tired or stressed. At these times, we are less likely to interpret objectively what is happening. The first maxim of facilitation should be: Facilitator, take care of thyself. Make sure to rest and eat well. Arrange for a group break to regenerate if necessary.

Will It Be Quick or Take Time?

Once a train has slowed, it requires extra energy to bring it back to speed. Once a group is idle, participants will begin off-topic conversations or mentally leave the room. The greater your repertoire of intervention strategies, the more extensive will be your choice of quick, one-stroke, brief corrections. The more credible the group finds you as a facilitator and the more mature as a group it is, the more permission you have to direct. Groups that have not reached a mature phase may require more explanations.

Can the Group Learn From It?

One way to extend a group's knowledge is by using a "process commercial," a brief statement of why you are using a particular intervention. To move beyond arguments about process, a facilitator might say, "There are no 'best' processes to prioritize, so instead of taking up time discussing the merits of different processes, let's just set this one in motion and see where we arrive."

INTERVENTION REPERTOIRE

Learning to facilitate requires continuously expanding your repertoire of facilitation strategies. Some common challenges and reliable interventions follow (Schwarz, 2002).

Redirect Conversation

Conversations can become abstract or, conversely, too mired in detail. Redirect conversations when they become unproductive by shifting the focus from one level to the other.

- "Susan, can you describe a time when that happened?"
- "Amit, can you give the group an example of that?"
- "Group, what seems to be the big idea here?"
- "Given these examples, what principles seem to be at work?"

Correct Problems by Using Abstract Examples

Make the example a broad statement or a hypothetical. By not pointing to an event or person, you reduce the group's or individual's defensiveness. For example, say:

- "When several conversations are occurring at the same time, it is difficult for everyone to hear."

Report Your Observations of Behavior

Sometimes the facilitator's neutral observation may be enough to alter the flow and the behavior. To deepen awareness, follow the statement of observation with a question that seeks to have the group direct:

- "Almost half the group is engaging in side talk. Is that OK with you?"
- "At our last meeting, we agreed to disagree agreeably. In the last conversation in this meeting, several

statements were made that presumed negative motivation from other group members. What language forms would you like to hear?"

■ "People seem tired. Is this correct? Do you want to take a break or do you want to push on for another 15 minutes?"

Intervene When an Individual's Behavior Is Counterproductive

Some behaviors are typical of groups.

■ *Broken record.* One person brings up the same point repeatedly. The individual may not feel he has been heard. First, paraphrase the person's comment, doing so several times if necessary. Match the tone of the participant's statement so he can be confident that both his idea and his emotion have been heard. A next step is to record the comment on a flip chart. If the person persists, move to the flip chart, paraphrase the statement again, and underline the written comment as you note, "Laurie, is this the idea you want to be sure the group understands?"

■ *Interrupting others.* Intervene immediately. Display an appropriate nonverbal sign like crossing your arms over your torso and saying, "Hang on, Linda. Let Faisal finish his thought."

■ *Boring the group.* Look for patterns. Person X speaks, and group members roll their eyes, look away, or seem embarrassed or disengaged. Later, person X speaks again and the reaction is the same. You need to help the group reduce this person's speaking time. Grinder (1996) suggests a strategy called Satisfy-Satisfy-Delay. Listen to the speaker a couple of times. When she next rises to speak, you delay . . . by not seeing, by calling on someone else, or by saying, "Maybe the group would like to hear from someone who hasn't spoken yet." Be sure to find a way to validate the person's contributions later.

- *Coming late.* The best way to have meetings start on time is to start on time. But with today's pressures, conflicts sometimes arise. Give members the benefit of the doubt. Try to have meetings begin with an activity or conversation that is valuable but not critical. Activating prior knowledge on a topic can serve this function nicely. If the same group member or members are consistently late, the group must address the issue.

- *Working on other tasks.* Busy hands aid listening. A doodler not disturbing the rest of the group may be OK. Leave the knitters alone; knitting can sometimes be an aid to listening. If the group seems distracted by someone working on a project, you might respectfully acknowledge the dilemma and ask if the person needs to work outside the group to complete a task. If several people are correcting papers or doing other organizational tasks, the facilitator must ask the group what about this meeting—its topic, dynamics, or processes—does not compel their attention. Another intervention is to direct people to sit with new partners for a conversation about the topic.

- *Isolating behavior.* One person always sits apart and does not want to be involved. Invite him to sit with the group. "David, here is a chair for you." If he declines, try again and move toward him to use body language to invite him forward. If he still refuses, say, "OK. Sitting there is an observation zone. When you want to participate, just move forward."

- *Talking to neighbors.* People talk on the side to check understanding, get ideas repeated, or share a response they don't feel comfortable reporting to the group. They comment to the person next to them because they are hot, cold, tired, and hungry. They comment because they agree—or because they disagree. If members consistently talk so they can work on other tasks, check calendars, or catch up socially, the group may need to build in structured time for these purposes.

One tip for beginning facilitators is to create an inventory on 3-by-5 cards of what you can do to intervene: interrupt and redirect a speaker, paraphrase at a higher logic level, report your observations of behavior, ask questions to illuminate perceptions about group performance or process, or modify the agenda. During your next opportunity to facilitate, note after each intervention what you are conscious of, your timing, and your results. Take time to reflect outside the meeting on what you are learning.

Perhaps the greatest challenge a facilitator faces is correcting individual or collective behaviors that detract from the group's work. Preparing to intervene and knowing when to do so are critical to effective facilitation. These strategies and principles of intervention will lead to more effective group behavior and enable the group to improve its work.

THREE RESPONSE STRATEGIES

When a facilitator is emotionally hooked by a group member's behavior or is uncertain how to respond, three strategies can help.

- Create an opportunity to move and breathe to get blood flowing back to the neocortex and away from the brain stem, allowing you to analyze the situation more objectively and move beyond judgment, blame, or defensiveness to a state of curiosity about the behavior.
- Have group members pair up to talk about a relevant topic and give you time to regroup.
- Remind yourself that most people are simply trying to take care of themselves, and try to figure out what positive intentions might be behind a behavior. People typically choose the best behavior available to them.

14

Setting Up the Room

Facilitating a group is a little like theater. You have a stage upon which you play, you have props, and you have a role to play. With experience, the facilitator becomes increasingly adept at managing all three.

SETTING THE STAGE

The work of the meeting begins well before the meeting starts. That may seem to state the obvious, but the facilitator has a key role in making sure the room is conducive to the group's work. Group members should walk onto a stage that has been set.

The room and its setup will affect group interaction and dynamics. The size of the room, the arrangement of the tables and chairs, the placement and types of materials, as well as their ready availability, all can aid or undermine the work of the most effective facilitator and most determined group.

Arrange the environment to support group learning. For example, form subgroups of those with diverse roles to promote discussion, and arrange the room so members' visual focus is on a chart rather than each other during problem-solving conversations. That puts problems out in the room and not with each other, making it more likely the group will have a civil discourse on tough topics.

Another point, although one that is not within our control to change, is the color of the room. While rooms cannot be repainted to suit the group, be aware of the effect of colors on the human subconscious. Room color can affect productivity. Greens and blues are good for discussion and engaging the team; blue, especially, promotes a relaxed feeling. Yellow helps with concentration, as long as the yellow is subtle and not overpowering in a small space. Sunny colors are cheerier, while physicians have found that red increases our pulse and breathing and raises blood pressure. Red increases risk-taking behavior. (Casinos use red in their décor.) Psychologists found that inmates in cells painted pink felt much calmer, although I cannot remember ever seeing a pink room in a school building. I've seen pink displays, however.

Room lighting can be an issue. Consider whether the room is sufficiently bright that the group can stay focused and whether it can be darkened enough if the group plans to use a media presentation. Note, too, where the outlets are for media as you plan the setup.

Use a room that is an appropriate size for the group. A group of five may find that the acoustics in the school media center aren't conducive to the work. Using a kindergarten room will ensure a meeting is short. One of the most uncomfortable meetings I've ever attended occurred in a classroom with child-sized chairs. Adult bodies are not meant to sit in them. In addition, classroom walls with a lot of visuals and displays can be distracting or make some feel anxious. Choose a room that will help the group meet its objectives.

Different room arrangements are better suited to different types of work. For example, an old-fashioned classroom setup is not as conducive to interaction as a simple round table.

Some room arrangements for small group work follow.

Hollow Square

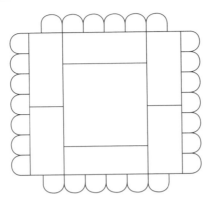

Arrangement: Tables arranged in a square or rectangle, with the center space open. Place chairs around the outside of the tables.

Group size: 12 to 20 people.

Benefits: Each person has a workspace and can see the rest of the group for conversation. Allows participants to feel equal and gives the facilitator spatial flexibility.

Best for: Group interaction, with a facilitator and recorder occupying the open space. Excellent for brainstorming and other activities requiring a public record.

U-Shape

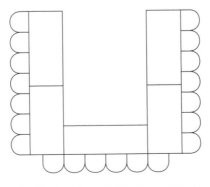

Arrangement: Tables placed end-to-end in the form of a U. Place chairs around the outside of the tables.

Group size: 8 to 20. (Making the sides longer for a larger group disrupts sight lines for conversation.)

Benefits: Allows individual workspace, and each participant can see the rest of the group for close interaction. Also creates a focal point at the open end of the U for the facilitator to work in. Allows participants to feel equal.

Best for: Small group conversation with facilitator interactions.

Alternative: Add chairs to the inside of the shape for additional seating. Be aware of disrupted sight lines and diminished work area.

Circle of Chairs

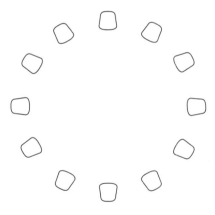

Arrangement: Circle of chairs.

Group size: 4 to 12.

Benefits: Each member may be fully involved without the unconscious barrier of a table between members. This setup is especially conducive to creating equality among participants.

Best for: Small group conversation that does not require work space in groups with high levels of trust; some may feel vulnerable in this configuration. Good for activities like grounding.

Conference Style

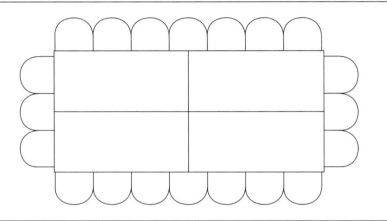

Arrangement: Place chairs around the outside of one or more tables.

Group size: 8 to 12 for round tables; 8 to 20 for single rectangular table or multiples placed together.

Benefits: Promotes small group interaction and discussion. Promotes unity with colleagues who are in close proximity and share the table. Allows members workspace.

Best for: Small groups without need for audio or visual presentation or a facilitator.

Large-group, presentation-style setups are shown in Appendix A.

TIPS

- Use a right-sized room.
- Review the meeting plan to decide on table arrangement.
- Allow at least 2 feet of work area for each group member.
- Plan what audiovisual materials will be needed.
- Set up tables and supplies 30 minutes ahead of time.
- Check that each person is able to see.
- Be available to greet people as they enter the room.

When preparing for a group meeting, consider the room's sound and visuals. Be aware of whether group members need to and will be able to see each other and what work space they will need. Try sitting and standing in different places to get a sense of how the setup will work. Look around and consider the effect of the elements in the room that can't change.

PROPS

When stage directors work with props, they take great care in selecting and placing the prop on the stage or in a waiting area.

Flip Charts

Visuals are essential for planning and problem-solving tasks. Flip charts can be used for visual reminders that help the group track ideas and aid in making decisions.

Flip charts are useful because they are readily available, relatively inexpensive aids for groups. Pages from the flip chart can be posted around the room as they are written on to prompt the group to remember past discussions, data, questions, and comments.

When the group needs to divide to work, flip chart pages are easy to use. Work groups can tear off a few pages and draw or write their separate notes. Most people are comfortable with a marker and paper, and informal charting can encourage participation.

Facilitators and recorders should note several best practices for using flip charts with a group:

- Print rather than writing in script.
- Use uppercase and lowercase, not all capital letters.
- Write large enough that all members can read from a distance.
- Alternate text colors.
- Try the rule of seven: Limit the number of words on each line and the number of lines on each page to seven.
- Use water-based, environmentally friendly markers. The fumes of some markers can be overwhelming. Even the popular scented markers can be distressing for some people.
- Be sure markers have large points for easier writing.
- Use sticky-backed paper, and place charts side by side rather than flipping them over on a board so that the information is always visible.
- Use a fresh page for a new topic or sketch.
- Leave room for more ideas at the bottom of each page.
- Keep your eyes on the chart as you record so as not to detract from the conversation or focus.
- Have the group clearly delineate how chart material will be corrected and what will not be recorded.
- Point to or stand beside the items as the group discusses them, and remain as still as possible. (Buckley, 2005)

Color can help chart viewers sort the various elements. In addition, to some extent, colors can guide emotional response. The way we respond to colors is partly cultural. For example, in the United States, green is often associated with finances. Colors can trigger unanticipated responses. If sketching people, make sure the figures are in a variety of colors. Darker colors are usually the most legible. Use a variety of colors for highlighting and making different points.

THE BEST COLORS FOR CHARTING

Some color tips for charting:

- For text, use strong, vibrant colors. Try alternating green, blue, and brown.
- Use red for headlines and organizers. People find it difficult to read a lot of red text, and it has negative connotations.
- Use black for boxes, arrows, and other graphic elements.
- Use yellow only sparingly as a highlight to draw attention or circle an item.
- Avoid light colors that can be difficult to see.

Hand out a summary of the flip chart notes to group members. A volunteer or the facilitator also can take digital photos of the posted pages and send them to participants to use as notes before the next meeting.

Interactive White Boards

The interactive white boards used in many classrooms today are good for capturing information that can be saved, stored, and easily distributed via e-mail. The interactive white board, however, can have a more formal feeling than the paper and marker flip chart for some generations in the group.

Figure 14.1   A Flip Chart or an Interactive White Board?

Flip Chart	Interactive White Board
Pages can be posted on walls during the meeting for easy viewing.	Not all pages can be visible at once.
Easy to use and amend (add on, circle, highlight, etc.)	Electronic expertise needed to use and amend.
Must be transcribed (with a potential for interpreting the material) or photographed in order to distribute.	Easy to record and maintain the record.
All can participate.	Some may find the technology intimidating.
Never runs out of power; few potential glitches.	Technical difficulties can stall its use.
Hand-drawn pictures and diagrams.	Can import pictures and access items from the Internet.
Clarity can be an issue.	Can be highly visible.

Some tips to remember if using the white board:

- White space is not wasted space. It is a visual help and organizer. Leave margins of 5 inches on all sides.
- Be sure to use the appropriate, nonpermanent markers.
- Use bright colors for easier visibility.

Technology Aids

Much technology is evolving that can assist facilitators and groups, from applications that can help in scheduling to online sharing and editing to recording information in the meeting. Doodle is a free tool for scheduling group meetings with the input of all group members. Doodle allows facilitators to poll group members to set a meeting time by creating a meeting title, selecting possible dates and times, inviting members to select those that work best for them, and then using the results to select the optimal time. Collaborative tools include Wikis,

Google Docs, or Sharepoint. Groups can share and work together on documents using commenting and discussion features.

Staff in meetings today often bring their mobile devices and laptops or iPads, using them either covertly or overtly. With the ready, almost ubiquitous, availability of this technology, put it to use. Rather than texting under the table, the meeting's recorder might tweet meeting information. An iPad application, Meeting Manager Pro, allows iPads to connect and documents to be projected on all the screens simultaneously, and provides interactive forms for creating surveys, votes, shared documents, and real-time feedback.

This chart neatly sums up some areas for facilitators to pay attention to as group members use their personal or school devices:

Enhancer	Inhibitor
Scheduling a meeting using Outlook or a similar scheduling tool	Neglecting to use the feature in the scheduling tool that lets you check availability of participants prior to sending the meeting request
When it's your turn to take meeting notes, capturing the gist of the meeting on an interactive whiteboard	When it's your turn to take meeting notes, capturing what you think should have been said rather than what was actually agreed upon
Using your PDA to quickly check your availability for the next meeting	Using your PDA to take notes and making everyone wait while you play the "I've almost got it . . ." game
Using your notebook to jot down personal notes in the meeting	Using your notebook to jot down your grocery list and favorite doodles during the meeting
Connecting your laptop to the network to capture notes directly or review relevant meeting material	Connecting your laptop to the network to read your e-mail during the meeting

Enhancer	Inhibitor
Using a projector to display information so that everyone in the room can follow	Using a projector and standing in front of the beam so that you look like you have a tattoo

Source: http://effectivemeetings.com

BODY LANGUAGE

The final element in the meeting is the facilitator. The facilitator is the ultimate prop. If the facilitator is nervous, the group will become nervous. If the facilitator is scattered, the group will not focus. If the facilitator is calm and confident, the work will proceed.

Effective communication relies on more than words. Research says that 60% to 70% of what we communicate is conveyed by our body language. When our words and our body language are in conflict, listeners receive mixed signals and tend to unconsciously both ascribe more truth to the body language and to assign the speaker less credibility and feel less trust because of the disconnect (Mehrabian, 2007).

People with nonverbal intelligence are systematic in their use of gesture, voice, breathing, and other nonverbal signals. Those with well-developed nonverbal intelligence quickly can establish rapport and choose which nonverbal skills to implement depending on the situation.

For example, my friend Kendall Zoller uses a video clip of Bill Clinton in some sessions to emphasize Clinton's posture. Clinton rests his hands on his knees. His shoulders are down. His posture conveys a sense of relaxation to the audience. Zoller's work on nonverbal patterns of communication is detailed in his 2010 book, *The Choreography of Presenting: The 7 Essential Abilities of Effective Presenters*.

MEETING CHECKLIST

Use this checklist to prepare for a meeting.

Equipment

- ❏ Flip chart
- ❏ LCD/BG projector and screen
- ❏ VCR and monitor
- ❏ Microphone (hand, lavaliere, cordless)
- ❏ Extension cord
- ❏ Other_____

Room Setup

- ❏ Room arrangement
- ❏ Refreshments
- ❏ Sign-in table
- ❏ Breakout room

Supplies

- ❏ Handouts
- ❏ Markers (water-based)
- ❏ Masking tape
- ❏ Sign-in sheet
- ❏ 3 x 5 cards
- ❏ Pencils or pens
- ❏ Scratch paper
- ❏ Music and player
- ❏ Other_____

Conclusion

At Birchwood School, the teachers, several support staff, members of the parents' advisory council, and the new principal all took part in intensive professional development. All of them committed to an after-school, on-site course in communication skills. The teachers received university credit, and a staff developer was paid to teach the course even though it was part of her regular work assignment. The faculty were so satisfied that they continued the course for two more semesters. Later, they also held a staff retreat, partially funded by the staff developer's pay for the course.

While these educators wanted to establish a whole-faculty group to work on improving communication, collaboration, and problem-solving, unexpected benefits appeared later. The district suffered an eight-day teacher strike. Birchwood was the only school to emerge from the strike with teacher-principal relationships intact and collaborative practices operational.

Not all team development is or needs to be as intensive as Birchwood's. Yet developing groups is as important as providing for individual growth. It may be more essential.

Studies consistently reveal that teacher behaviors, attitudes, and knowledge are influenced more by the workplace culture than the skills, knowledge, training, and backgrounds of individual teachers.

CREATE AN EFFECTIVE GROUP

Capable groups are made, not born. Working communities grow, learn from experience, and become more productive. In less effective schools, things stay the same, group learning is episodic, and the capacity of educators to work together to improve teaching remains relatively static.

Where do groups begin in order to learn to be more effective? Each group is unique. The school setting, the group's tasks, members' histories, and mental models all combine to create a team with a distinct personality. Variables, such as collective efficacy, craftsmanship, and consciousness influence not only a group's effectiveness but also its ability to develop further.

As evidence mounts that student learning is the result of collaborative effort, teachers will increasingly need skills to conduct productive meetings in which they generate the know-how and will to do the right work to improve instruction, raise student achievement, and enhance professional community. However, creating such cultures of inquiry and developing productive groups is much easier said than done.

Over the last decade, we have learned that restructuring efforts are useful but not sufficient to improve learning. Sadly, through initiatives in several states, we also have discovered that assigning money and control to the school level led to changes at some schools, but no changes in most schools, let alone to improvements in student learning (Joyce, 2004). We also know that even well-structured professional development initiatives are ineffective when they lack practical follow-through phases in which applications are practiced, self-assessed, and modified.

To begin to create an environment in which teachers effectively use collaborative skills to conduct productive meetings about student learning requires training. Teachers are fine learners and, under the proper conditions, put learning to work. When they know how to do something, they do it. Yet teachers most often work in isolation, and professional learning programs seldom invest time in teaching teachers to work with other adults. Professional development in this area is a must.

For some time, educators have had a chicken-or-egg argument regarding professional development. Does commitment come before competence—or the other way around? My sense is that both are true.

During a visit to Southeast Asia, I was struck by the extent and variety of teacher collaboration on such activities as developing benchmarks and assessments to meet standards, producing unit plans, and reflecting on student work. In two International School Districts, one in Kuala Lumpur and the other in Jakarta, teachers and administrators worked together to accomplish these tasks and improve their collaboration skills.

How do schools such as these sustain innovation? Initially, of course, they must experience innovation. To do this, most members need to have new behaviors, practices, and ways of thinking about their work permeate their activities.

This book may help school groups to develop those necessary new behaviors that lead to new practices. Developing productive groups will become increasingly important as teacher groups take the forefront in the work that must occur to improve student achievement. We can facilitate the effectiveness of this effort by helping teachers learn to work collaboratively with other adults and to build their capability for self-reflection and self-assessment. Groups whose members commit to these principles will be productive.

Appendixes

Appendix A

Large Group Room Configurations

One facilitation tip I've picked up that can improve group interaction is to have fewer chairs set up in the room than the number of people you expect. Put a stack of extra chairs off to the side so they are accessible if they are needed. Consider putting them at the front to fill in the front of the room. Having fewer chairs than the expected number of people does not allow the group to spread out as much. Having people sitting closer together, and closer to the front of the room, will increase energy in the room.

Some set ups for large groups are:

Classroom Style

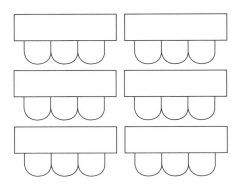

Arrangement: Arrange rows of tables with two to three chairs at each. Allow 3 to 3 ½ feet between rows for optimum movement. Two or three columns are best.

Group size: Limited by room size.

Benefits: Facilitator can see participants. Maximizes use of space for larger groups. Allows work space for taking notes or referencing materials.

Best for: Large groups where interaction is minimal and participants' primary function is to approve or disapprove ideas placed before them.

Clusters

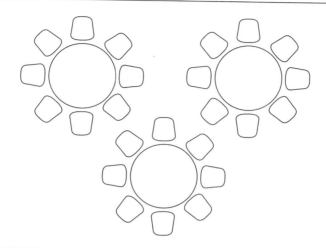

Arrangement: Round tables placed with six to eight chairs around each.

Group size: 60 to 100. Meetings of this size need to be highly structured, and often the outcomes might be limited to developing understanding or skills or approving or denying proposals put before the full group. The Focusing Four is one exception to this limitation on large group outcomes. I've done it with groups as large as 200.

Benefits: Allows for small group discussion and work.

Best for: Conducive to breakout group work, as well as whole group participation.

Herringbone

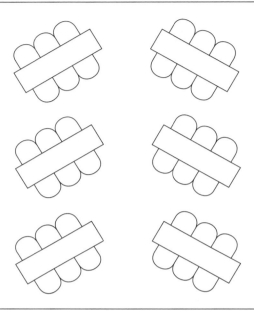

Arrangement: Tables placed tilted toward the front center point of the room, forming an upside down V figure. Can be two or three rows, with two rows ideal. Place four to six chairs at each table. Whenever possible, position the back of the room adjacent to the entry door to reduce distractions during the meeting.

Group size: 25 to 75.

Benefits: Allows discussion among small groups of participants during or immediately after a larger group activity. Creates a more enclosed feel for a presenter and audience.

Best for: An informational meeting with some audience dialogue.

Appendix B

Sample Inventory

*Five Energy Sources for High
Performing Groups*

Efficacy

Behavioral Indicators:	1	2	3	4

The decisions we make usually stay made.

Our team's work impacts important issues.

The goals of our team have real meaning for us.

We draw on our experience and use the knowledge and skills we have to be an effective team.

Flexibility

Behavioral Indicators:	1	2	3	4

We adjust our work during meetings to be more effective.

As we think about specific issues, we expand our thinking to encompass a larger view.

Flexibility (Continued)

Behavioral Indicators:	1	2	3	4

We view situations through our own eyes and the eyes of others.

We consider several ways of doing something before deciding what might work best.

We consider the impact of our work and our decisions before we act.

Craftsmanship

Behavioral Indicators:	1	2	3	4

We are good at predicting and managing time.

We strive to improve the ways we do things.

Our communication with each other is clear.

We accomplish what we hope to in most of our meetings.

We home in on issues and look at the specific facts relevant to the issue.

Consciousness

Behavioral Indicators:	1	2	3	4

We pay attention to team development and group process.

We are aware of where we are in our work and where we want to be with our work.

We know why we are a team.

We can articulate the processes we use (for example, decision making and problem solving) and know who is accountable for what.

We use what we have learned to make us more effective.

Interdependence

Behavioral Indicators:	1	2	3	4
We have common goals and values.				
We are aware of organizational goals with which we must coordinate our team's goals.				
Members are supportive of the team's efforts and decisions.				
We work well together.				
We each feel valued as members of this team.				

Source: Ellison & Hayes, 1999. Used by permission.

The full instrument includes 12 questions for each energy source and provides a score that groups can use for item analysis and to set goals. Copies of the full instrument can be ordered from www.adaptiveschools.com.

Appendix C

Seven Norms of Collaboration: A Supporting Toolkit

Mark Ravlin (Mark@viamandala.com)

The Norms of Collaboration	The Tools
1. Pausing	◆ Norms of Collaboration
2. Paraphrasing	◆ Norms of Collaboration: Annotated
3. Posing Questions	◆ Rating the Consistency of My Personal Behavior in a Specific Group...
4. Putting Ideas on the Table	◆ Checking Personal Consistency or Summarizing Personal Ratings
5. Providing Data	◆ Rating the Consistency of Group Member Behavior
6. Paying Attention to Self and Others	◆ Checking Group Member Consistency or Summarizing Member Ratings
7. Presuming Positive Intentions	

This Toolkit is designed to provide resources for developing and sustaining productive group interaction through the practice of seven *Norms of Collaboration.* Consistent use of these norms enhances the quality and productivity of all forms of conversation in any group. More extensive explanation and ideas for initiating their use can be found in chapter two of *The Adaptive School: A Sourcebook for Developing Collaborative Groups* (Garmston and Wellman, 2009, pp. 27-43).

Topics

Using the Tools
1. Introducing the Norms
2. Posting the Norms
3. Sustaining Engagement with the Norms
4. Assessing Consistency with the Norms
   - 4.1 Norms Inventory: *Rating the Consistency of My Personal Behavior in a Specific Group of Which I am a Member*
     - 4.1a Solo Use
     - 4.1b Combining Solo with Group Use
   - 4.2 Norms Inventory: *Rating the Consistency of Group Member Behavior*
     - 4.2a Solo Use
     - 4.2b Combining Solo with Group Use – At the Table
     - 4.2c Combining Solo with Group Use – On the Wall
5. Norms Inventories: Introductory Applications
   - 5.1 Using Checking Personal Consistency... for Introductory Assessment

Guidelines and Considerations

www.adaptiveschools.com

Using the Tools

1. Introducing the *Norms*

One common method for introducing the *Norms of Collaboration* is to create a shared reading process, using the annotated edition that defines and exemplifies the norms. Group members then engage in reflective conversations about the reading, in pairs or table groups, guided by questions such as the following.

- "What personal connections are you making with this set of norms?"
- "Which of these norms might be most important for your full participation in a group?"
- "Considering these seven norms, which might you find most challenging?"
- "Given your selection, what strategies might you use to focus on this/these?"

2. Posting the *Norms*

Once the *Norms of Collaboration* are introduced, facilitators often post them, creating a third point source of habits for the group. Consider the facilitator to be the first point, the group to be the second point. The norms text in poster form serves as a third point, separate from each of the others. This provides psychological safety for the group to talk about the norms independent of the facilitator: their source is separate and clear for all to see.

3. Sustaining Engagement with the *Norms*

In addition, experienced facilitators often provide each individual with a copy of the annotated edition of the *Norms*, and request that they bring them to each meeting. An additional reminding strategy is to provide each table with a master copy at each meeting, which members see as they arrive. Effective groups address the *Norms* as part of opening and closing most meetings. Opening activities often ask individuals or groups to select one or two norms for particular focus during the session. Closing activities may ask individuals to reflect on decisions they made regarding the focus norm(s), and effects they observed.

4. Assessing Consistency with the Norms

4.1 Norms Inventory: *Rating the Consistency of My Personal Behavior in a Specific Group of Which I am a Member*

"There is no such thing as group behavior. All 'group behavior' results from the decisions and actions of individuals. When individual choices align in productive patterns, the group generates positive results (Garmston and Wellman, 1999, p. 33)." Group development is enhanced as individual group members become more conscious of and skillful with the behaviors that comprise the *Norms of Collaboration*.

This tool guides individual group members in assessing analytically the consistency with which they practice the behavior that is promoted by each of the seven norms. The *Inventory* includes twenty-one behaviors, three for each of the seven norms, asking that individual participants rate themselves as members of a specific group that a facilitator names – perhaps the present group, or others in participants' work sites.

4.1a   Solo Use

The personal behavior inventory may be used on its own, "solo," when the facilitator's purpose is to enhance the identified group's functioning by focusing individual members on their behavioral choices in the group. In this case, the facilitator asks each group member to complete an *Inventory*, per its instructions – naming the specific group. Pairs or table groups then reflect on such questions as,

- "What are you noticing about your perceptions?"

In some circumstances, a facilitator may want the group to reflect on the behavior of a specific norm or two – for example paraphrasing, so the inquiry might be,

- "Considering paraphrasing, what were you paying attention to as you rated yourself on each of the types?"

Either of these might be followed with a growth-focused question such as,

- "What strategies might you use to increase your consistency ratings?"

4.1b   Combining Solo with Group Use

The personal behavior inventory may also be combined with the tool called *Checking Personal Consistency / Summarizing Personal Ratings*. After individuals complete their personal behavior inventories, they summarize their results by estimating the average of the three scores for each norm, marking their averages on a copy of *Checking Personal Consistency / Summarizing Personal Ratings*. This permits ensuing conversation to include both behavioral references from the personal behavior inventory, as well as more general reference to the norms from the summarized, or averaged, scores. A common guiding question for either pairs or table groups is,

- "What are you noticing about the consistency with which you are practicing the *Norms of Collaboration*?"

This might be followed with a growth-focused question such as,

- "What might be important ways for you to increase your consistency ratings?"

4.2 Norms Inventory: *Rating the Consistency of Group Member Behavior*

This tool guides individual group members, the group as a whole, and table groups when these are present, in assessing the consistency with which group members practice the behaviors that are associated with the seven *Norms of Collaboration*.

4.2a   Solo Use

The *Group Member Behavior Inventory* may be used on its own – by a work group, a table group in a larger group context, or a large group – when the facilitator's assessment is that the group's productivity will be enhanced by individual members taking a group perspective on the behavior of all of the individual members, at the analytic level. The focus is behavioral; the attention is on the "we" of the group. The facilitator asks each member to complete a *Group Member Behavior* inventory per its instructions. Pairs or table groups then reflect on questions such as,

- "What are you noticing in your data about the group's members?"
- "What meaning might you be making, as you consider your data about the group?"

4.2b   Combining Solo with Group Use – At the Table

A. The *Group Member Behavior Inventory* may also be used with the tool for *Checking Group Member Consistency / Summarizing Member Ratings*, when the facilitator's assessment is that the group would benefit from viewing the members' data at the normative level – in contrast to the behavioral level above. When individuals have completed their *Group Member Behavior* inventories, each summarizes their data by estimating the averages of their ratings on a *Checking Group Member Consistency / Summarizing Member Ratings* tool. In this process, each group member collates data individually. The facilitator may then ask that pairs or table groups reflect on their data about how consistently the norms are practiced in the group. A common guiding question is,

- "What observations are you making about the group members' practice of the norms?"

B. The facilitator's assessment may be that the group would benefit from considering its members' data in a format in which all of the information is included in a single view. In such cases, the facilitator may ask the group to combine the norms data of each individual on a single *Checking Group Member Consistency / Summarizing Member Ratings* tool. Members mark their respective estimated averages on a group copy of the tool, each in a different color. The facilitator may guide reflection on these data with questions such as,

- "What are your observations about the group's perceptions?"

The facilitator might follow this with a growth-focused question such as,

- "What norm(s) might the group focus on, to increase its productivity and satisfaction?"
  - "Given the potential of focusing on (a norm), what strategies might group members use to accomplish this?"

At this point, the facilitator may choose to ask the group to commit to a specific focus of improvement, based on this conversation. In this event, it is important that the facilitator return to the commitment toward the conclusion of the meeting, to provide group members with an opportunity to reflect on the results of their improvement focus.

4.2c   Combining Solo with Group Use – On the Wall

A facilitator may make the assessment that a group's purpose(s) may be served, and/or its productivity increased, by public consideration of its norms data. This can be accomplished in at least two ways. In both, the norms data of the group are posted on the wall. This has the effect of distancing the data from the group to a third point, which can increase the psychological safety to engage in conversation about the data.

A. This process is a variation on <u>Combining Solo and Group Use – At the Table</u>, described above. Instead of combining the individuals' norms data onto a single *Checking Group Member Consistency / Summarizing Member Ratings* tool in its standard size, each group is provided with a piece of chart paper. The facilitator asks that a recorder in each group recreate the scales of the *Checking Group Member Consistency / Summarizing Member Ratings* tool on the chart paper, in black. Members then mark their respective estimated averages on the chart edition of *Checking Group Member Consistency / Summarizing Member Ratings* tool, using a different color for each member. The facilitator then guides consideration of the data with inquiries similar to those above.

B. A facilitator may use this opportunity to create a more structured study of group data. This can be done by following the process described in 1, just above, with the following addition.

The facilitator introduces the process of *Here's What!, So What?, Now What?* to guide the group's consideration of the data. This process uses a three-column protocol, illustrated below. The intention is to support a group in describing <u>what they see</u> in the data (*Here's What!*), then and separately considering the <u>meanings</u> of the data (*So What?*), and finally what <u>actions</u> the group might take (*Now What?*). This process is particularly helpful to groups that need to learn to observe data, separately from assigning meaning, and to hold off on action planning until their study of the data is complete. More extensive description and explanation of this process and others related to the study of data can be found in *Data-Driven Dialogue* (Wellman and Lipton, 2004). www.miravia.com).

Here's What!	So What?	Now What?

5. Norms Inventories: Introductory Applications

The applications of the norms inventories described above begin with individuals rating their personal consistency or that of group members analytically, at the behavioral level. The behavioral perceptions data may then be averaged to yield summaries at the level of the seven *Norms*.

Beginning with behavioral ratings permits highly focused conversation, which a facilitator may assess to be of particular importance in advancing a group's effectiveness. It also calls for significant knowledge about each of the norms, such as the three purposes for paraphrasing – to acknowledge and clarify, to summarize and organize, and to shift levels of abstraction. It also calls for a significant investment of group time, ever in short supply in school settings.

Assessing consistency with the *Norms* can also begin at the normative level, as early as when a group first becomes familiar with the *Norms*. Facilitators find this approach useful for introducing self-assessment early in the process of learning and applying the Norms, with groups that are not yet fully versed in the key concepts and behaviors associated with the *Norms*, and when time is at a premium.

5.1 Using *Checking Personal Consistency/ Summarizing Personal Ratings* for Introductory Assessment

After introducing the Norms (Section 1), the facilitator invites each participant to estimate levels of personal consistency with the tool for *Checking Personal Consistency / Summarizing Personal Ratings*. This may be done individually only (see Section 4.1a), supported by pairs or table group conversation.

It may also be extended into combining the individual data into a group display and conversation (see Section 4.1b). This might also be extended to posting the group's data, as in section 5.2c. Facilitators often use such a public third point display of the data to inform a group's conversation about which norm or two the group might focus on to improve its members' consistency and the group's performance.

As groups construct deeper knowledge and more become more consistent in their use of the Norms, experienced facilitators often increase the specificity of subsequent self-assessment activities by shifting to the *Rating the Consistency of My Personal Behavior…* tool, described in section 4.1 above.

Guidelines and Considerations

Using the Consistency Scales

One scale is used repeatedly in all of the rating tools.

The scale is designed for flexibility and estimation. Facilitators encourage group members to use the scale to best reflect their perceptions. The numbers on the scale describe ranges (1, 2, 3, 4). One member's perception may be a "low 2." This person would make a mark somewhere to the left of the number 2 and to the right of the crossbar below it. Another member may perceive a "high 3." The corresponding mark would be placed to the right of the number 3 and to the left of the crossbar above it. Facilitators may find it helpful to advise group members to not over-think their responses; one's first inclination is likely to be important.

Estimating Averages

Given the flexibility of the consistency scale, precise mathematical calculation of averages would not be suitable. Facilitators should be explicit about this, and be prepared to support group members who are accustomed to considering numbers only with calculator in-hand.

Working Agreements Complement the Norms

The *Norms of Collaboration* are based on decades of research and practice in the fields of counseling, coaching, group dynamics, facilitation, and professional learning communities. They constitute best practice throughout these fields, with results documented in both education (Kennedy, A., Deuel, A., Nelson, T, and Slavit, D. "Requiring Collaboration or Distributing Leadership?" *Phi Delta Kappan*, Vol, 92, No. 8, 2011, pp. 20-24) and business (Losada, M. and Heaphy, E. "The Role of Positivity and Connectivity in Performance of Business Teams: A Nonlinear Dynamic Model," *American Behavioral Scientist*, Vol. 47, No. 6, 2004, pp. 740-765).

Working Agreements, on the other hand, are specific to a group. They define the expected behavior among group members in areas that the members decide will support their effectiveness in reaching important outcomes. Like the *Norms of Collaboration*, they are based on beliefs, values, and consensus among group members. An experienced facilitator assesses when to engage a group in defining areas that call for the support of *Working Agreements*, and in developing the language that the group's members support.

In some situations, the *Working Agreements* may be for long-term use by the group, in which case they are posted alongside the *Norms of Collaboration*. Under other circumstances, they may be developed for a specific meeting. Common themes addressed by *Working Agreements* are focus on the topic-at-hand, respecting all members' points of view, starting and ending on time, and being prepared for meetings.

Working Agreements become effective as the members of a group engage in their development, and regularly self-assess to assure that group members' behavioral choices and decisions align with the *Agreements*. They are not called for in all groups. Experienced facilitators learn to observe and interpret the performance of a group's members, as the basis of a decision to engage the members in developing *Working Agreements*. It is essential that the processes for developing and supporting them engage members in ways that build shared ownership.

Consistent Attention to the *Norms of Collaboration* and *Working Agreements*

Group productivity and satisfaction increase with growth in the consistency with which group members practice the behaviors that are associated with the *Norms of Collaboration* and the group's *Working Agreements*. The *Norms* are intended for use among group members both in meetings and in general, whereas *Working Agreements* pertain to members' behavior in the group's meetings. Realizing the collaborative potential of the *Norms* and *Working Agreements* requires consistent and repeated attention. Facilitators develop a repertoire of ways to address the *Norms* and the group's *Agreements*, so that this can become a regular opening and closing event at most or all group meetings.

Norms of Collaboration

1. Pausing

2. Paraphrasing

3. Posing Questions

4. Putting Ideas on the Table

5. Providing Data

6. Paying Attention to Self and Others

7. Presuming Positive Intentions

Norms of Collaboration
Annotated

1. Pausing
Pausing before responding or asking a question allows time for thinking and enhances dialogue, discussion, and decision-making.

2. Paraphrasing
Using a paraphrase starter that is comfortable for you – "So…" or "As you are…" or "You're thinking…" – and following the starter with an efficient paraphrase assists members of the group in hearing and understanding one another as they converse and make decisions.

3. Posing Questions
Two intentions of posing questions are to explore and to specify thinking. Questions may be posed to explore perceptions, assumptions, and interpretations, and to invite others to inquire into their thinking. For example, "What might be some conjectures you are exploring?" Use focusing questions such as, "Which students, specifically?" or "What might be an example of that?" to increase the clarity and precision of group members' thinking. Inquire into others' ideas before advocating one's own.

4. Putting Ideas on the Table
Ideas are the heart of meaningful dialogue and discussion. Label the intention of your comments. For example: "Here is one idea…" or "One thought I have is…" or "Here is a possible approach…" or "Another consideration might be…".

5. Providing Data
Providing data, both qualitative and quantitative, in a variety of forms supports group members in constructing shared understanding from their work. Data have no meaning beyond that which we make of them; shared meaning develops from collaboratively exploring, analyzing, and interpreting data.

6. Paying Attention to Self and Others
Meaningful dialogue and discussion are facilitated when each group member is conscious of self and of others, and is aware of what (s)he is saying <u>and</u> how it is said as well as how others are responding. This includes paying attention to learning styles when planning, facilitating, and participating in group meetings and conversations.

7. Presuming Positive Intentions
Assuming that others' intentions are positive promotes and facilitates meaningful dialogue and discussion, and prevents unintentional put-downs. Using positive intentions in speech is one manifestation of this norm.

Norms Inventory

Rating the Consistency of My Personal Behavior
In a Specific Group of Which I am a Member

Place a mark on each scale, to reflect your perception of your personal behavior in a specified group of which you are a member.

1. Pausing

A. I pause after asking questions.

Low ●———┼———┼———┼———● High
     1   2   3   4

B. I pause after others speak to reflect before responding.

Low ●———┼———┼———┼———● High
     1   2   3   4

C. I pause before asking questions to permit thoughtful construction.

Low ●———┼———┼———┼———● High
     1   2   3   4

2. Paraphrasing

A. I listen and paraphrase to acknowledge and clarify.

Low ●———┼———┼———┼———● High
     1   2   3   4

B I listen and paraphrase to summarize and organize.

Low ●———┼———┼———┼———● High
     1   2   3   4

C. I listen and paraphrase to shift levels of abstraction.

Low ●———┼———┼———┼———● High
     1   2   3   4

3. Posing Questions

A. I pose questions to explore perceptions, assumptions, and interpretations.

Low ●———┼———┼———┼———● High
     1   2   3   4

B. I inquire before putting my ideas on the table, or advocating.

Low ●———┼———┼———┼———● High
     1   2   3   4

C. I seek specificity of data, assumptions, generalizations, and the meaning of words.

Low ●———┼———┼———┼———● High
     1   2   3   4

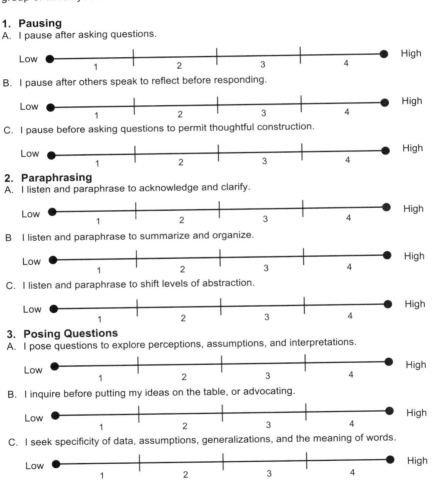

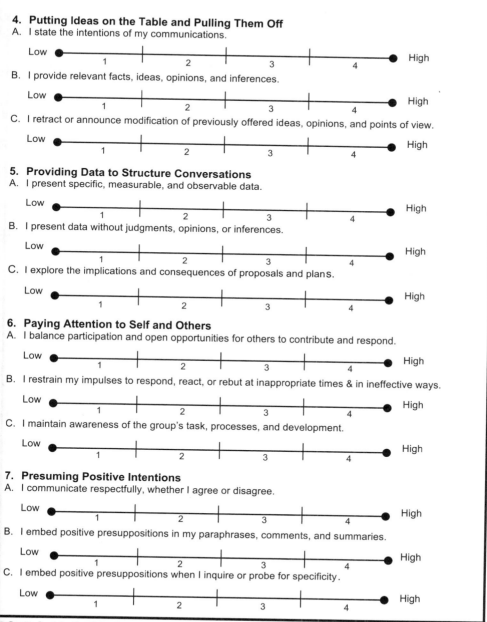

4. Putting Ideas on the Table and Pulling Them Off
A. I state the intentions of my communications.
B. I provide relevant facts, ideas, opinions, and inferences.
C. I retract or announce modification of previously offered ideas, opinions, and points of view.

5. Providing Data to Structure Conversations
A. I present specific, measurable, and observable data.
B. I present data without judgments, opinions, or inferences.
C. I explore the implications and consequences of proposals and plans.

6. Paying Attention to Self and Others
A. I balance participation and open opportunities for others to contribute and respond.
B. I restrain my impulses to respond, react, or rebut at inappropriate times & in ineffective ways.
C. I maintain awareness of the group's task, processes, and development.

7. Presuming Positive Intentions
A. I communicate respectfully, whether I agree or disagree.
B. I embed positive presuppositions in my paraphrases, comments, and summaries.
C. I embed positive presuppositions when I inquire or probe for specificity.

Norms of Collaboration
Checking Personal Consistency
or Summarizing Personal Ratings

Place a mark on each scale to reflect your perception of your behavior.

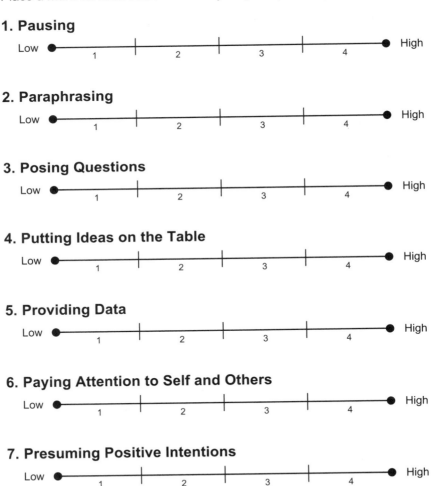

1. Pausing

Low ●————|————|————|————● High
     1   2   3   4

2. Paraphrasing

Low ●————|————|————|————● High
     1   2   3   4

3. Posing Questions

Low ●————|————|————|————● High
     1   2   3   4

4. Putting Ideas on the Table

Low ●————|————|————|————● High
     1   2   3   4

5. Providing Data

Low ●————|————|————|————● High
     1   2   3   4

6. Paying Attention to Self and Others

Low ●————|————|————|————● High
     1   2   3   4

7. Presuming Positive Intentions

Low ●————|————|————|————● High
     1   2   3   4

     www.adaptiveschools.com

Norms Inventory
Rating the Consistency of Group Member Behavior

Place a mark on each scale, to reflect your perception of the behavior of group members.

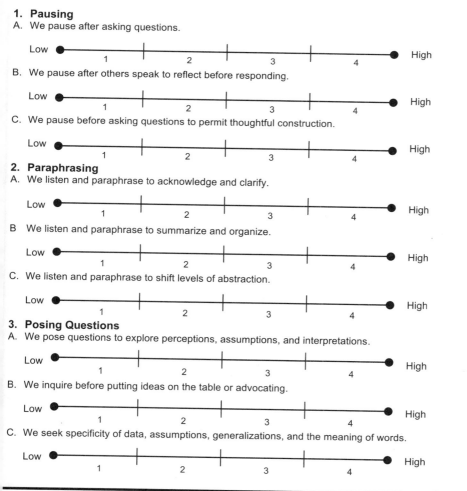

1. Pausing
A. We pause after asking questions.

Low ●———————|————————|————————|————————● High
　　　　1　　　　　2　　　　　3　　　　　4

B. We pause after others speak to reflect before responding.

Low ●———————|————————|————————|————————● High
　　　　1　　　　　2　　　　　3　　　　　4

C. We pause before asking questions to permit thoughtful construction.

Low ●———————|————————|————————|————————● High
　　　　1　　　　　2　　　　　3　　　　　4

2. Paraphrasing
A. We listen and paraphrase to acknowledge and clarify.

Low ●———————|————————|————————|————————● High
　　　　1　　　　　2　　　　　3　　　　　4

B We listen and paraphrase to summarize and organize.

Low ●———————|————————|————————|————————● High
　　　　1　　　　　2　　　　　3　　　　　4

C. We listen and paraphrase to shift levels of abstraction.

Low ●———————|————————|————————|————————● High
　　　　1　　　　　2　　　　　3　　　　　4

3. Posing Questions
A. We pose questions to explore perceptions, assumptions, and interpretations.

Low ●———————|————————|————————|————————● High
　　　　1　　　　　2　　　　　3　　　　　4

B. We inquire before putting ideas on the table or advocating.

Low ●———————|————————|————————|————————● High
　　　　1　　　　　2　　　　　3　　　　　4

C. We seek specificity of data, assumptions, generalizations, and the meaning of words.

Low ●———————|————————|————————|————————● High
　　　　1　　　　　2　　　　　3　　　　　4

　　　　　　　　www.adaptiveschools.com

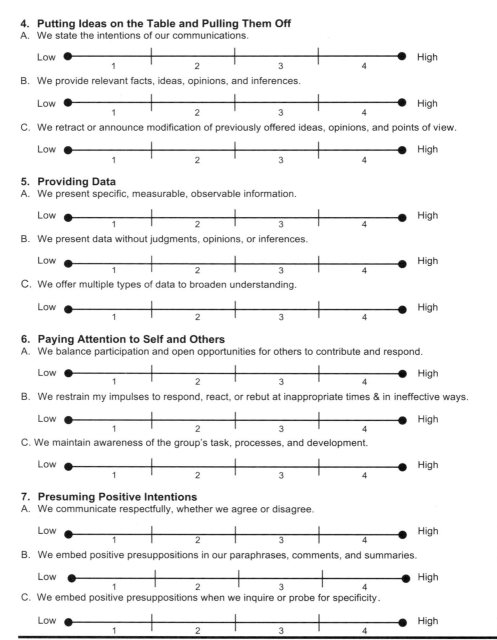

4. Putting Ideas on the Table and Pulling Them Off
A. We state the intentions of our communications.

Low ● 1 2 3 4 ● High

B. We provide relevant facts, ideas, opinions, and inferences.

Low ● 1 2 3 4 ● High

C. We retract or announce modification of previously offered ideas, opinions, and points of view.

Low ● 1 2 3 4 ● High

5. Providing Data
A. We present specific, measurable, observable information.

Low ● 1 2 3 4 ● High

B. We present data without judgments, opinions, or inferences.

Low ● 1 2 3 4 ● High

C. We offer multiple types of data to broaden understanding.

Low ● 1 2 3 4 ● High

6. Paying Attention to Self and Others
A. We balance participation and open opportunities for others to contribute and respond.

Low ● 1 2 3 4 ● High

B. We restrain my impulses to respond, react, or rebut at inappropriate times & in ineffective ways.

Low ● 1 2 3 4 ● High

C. We maintain awareness of the group's task, processes, and development.

Low ● 1 2 3 4 ● High

7. Presuming Positive Intentions
A. We communicate respectfully, whether we agree or disagree.

Low ● 1 2 3 4 ● High

B. We embed positive presuppositions in our paraphrases, comments, and summaries.

Low ● 1 2 3 4 ● High

C. We embed positive presuppositions when we inquire or probe for specificity.

Low ● 1 2 3 4 ● High

Norms of Collaboration
Checking Group Member Consistency
or Summarizing Member Ratings

Place a mark on each scale to reflect your perception of group members' behavior.

1. Pausing

Low  High
1   2   3   4

2. Paraphrasing

Low  High
1   2   3   4

3. Posing Questions

Low  High
1   2   3   4

4. Putting Ideas on the Table

Low  High
1   2   3   4

5. Providing Data

Low  High
1   2   3   4

6. Paying Attention to Self and Others

Low  High
1   2   3   4

7. Presuming Positive Intentions

Low  High
1   2   3   4

www.adaptiveschools.com

References

Achinstein, B. (2002). Conflict amid community: The micropolitics of teacher collaboration. *Teachers College Record, 104*(3), 421–455.

Albert, S., & Whetten, D. A. (1985). Organizational identity. In L. L. Cummings & B. M. Staw (Eds.), *Research in organizational behavior* (Vol. 7, pp. 263–295). Greenwich, CT: JAI Press.

Amason, A., Thompson, K., Hochwater, W., & Harrison, A. (1995). Conflict: An important dimension in successful management teams. *Organizational Dynamics, 24*(2), 20–35.

Berliner, D. (1988, February). The development of expertise in pedagogy. Paper presented at the meeting of the American Association of Colleges for Teacher Education, New Orleans, LA.

Briggs, J. (1992). *Fractals: The patterns of chaos.* New York: Touchstone Books.

Bryk, A., & Schneider, B. (2004). *Trust in schools: A core resource for improvement.* Volume in the American Sociological Association's Rose Series in Sociology. New York: Russell Sage Foundation.

Buckley, M. (2005). To see is to retain. In R. J. Garmston (Ed.), *The presenter's fieldbook: A practical guide* (2nd ed., pp. 181–204). Norwood, MA: Christopher-Gordon.

Canetti, E. (1960). *Crowds and power.* New York: Farrar, Straus, and Giroux.

Capra, F. (1991). *The Tao of physics.* Boston: Shambhala Publications.

Christakis, N. A., & Fowler, J. H. (2009). *Connected: The surprising power of our social networks and how they shape our lives.* New York: Little, Brown.

Costa, A. (1985). Toward a model of intellectual functioning. In A. Costa (Ed.), *Developing minds: A resource book for teaching thinking.* Alexandria, VA: Association for Supervision and Curriculum Development.

Costa, A., & Garmston, R. J. (2002). *Cognitive coaching: A foundation for Renaissance schools.* Norwood, MA: Christopher-Gordon.

Crum, T. (1997). *The magic of conflict: Turning a life of work into a work of art.* New York: Touchstone.

Devall, B., & Sessions, G. (1985). *Deep ecology: Living as if nature mattered.* Layton, UT: Peregrine Smith Books.

Doyle, M., & Strauss, D. (1976). *How to make meetings work!* New York: Berkley Books.

DuFour, R. (2004). What is a professional learning community? *Educational Leadership, 61*(8), 6–11.

Ellison, J., & Hayes, C. (1999). Five energy sources for high performing groups. In R. J. Garmston & B. Wellman, *The adaptive school: A sourcebook for developing collaborative groups.* Norwood, MA: Christopher-Gordon.

Fabre, J.-H. (1916). The pine processionary: The procession. In *The life of caterpillars.* Retrieved from http://www.efabre.net/chapter-iii-the-pine-processionary-the-procession.

Fredrickson, B. L., & Losada, M. F. (2005). Positive affect and the complex dynamics of human flourishing. *American Psychologist, 60*(7), 678–686.

Forsyth, P., Adams, C., & Hoy, W. (2011). *Collective trust: Why schools can't improve without it.* Thousand Oaks, CA: Corwin.

Frymier, J. (1987). Bureaucracy and the neutering of teachers. *Phi Delta Kappan, 69*(1), 9–14.

Garmston, R. J. (2003). The leader creates a vision of what the group can become. *Journal of Staff Development, 24*(3).

Garmston, R. J. (2006). The 5 principles of effective meetings. *The Learning System, 1*(4), 6–8.

Garmston, R. J. (2008a). Four mental aptitudes help facilitators facing challenges. *Journal of Staff Development, 29*(1), 65–66.

Garmston, R. J. (2008b). Use "both/and" thinking to find the best of two sides of a conflict. *Journal of Staff Development, 29*(4), 49–50.

Garmston, R. J., & Dolcemascolo, M. (2009). *An introduction to dialogue.* [DVD with Viewers Guide.] Highlands Ranch, CO: Center for Adaptive Schools.

Garmston, R. J., & Hyerle, D. (1988, August). *Professors' peer coaching program.* Sacramento, CA: California State University.

Garmston, R. J., & Welch, D. (2007). Results-oriented agendas transform meetings into valuable collaborative events. *Journal of Staff Development, 28*(2), 55–56.

Garmston, R. J., & Wellman, B. (1995). Adaptive schools in a quantum universe. *Educational Leadership, 52*(7), 6–12.

Garmston, R. J., & Wellman, B. (1998). Teacher talk that makes a difference. *Educational Leadership, 55*(7), 30–34.

Garmston, R. J., & Wellman, B. (2002). *The adaptive school: Developing and facilitating collaborative groups: Syllabus* (4th ed.). Norwood, MA: Christopher-Gordon.

Garmston, R. J., & Wellman, B. (2009). *The adaptive school: A sourcebook for developing collaborative groups* (2nd ed.). Norwood, MA: Christopher-Gordon.

Gherardi, S., & Nicolini, D. (2002). Learning in a constellation of interconnected practices: Canon or dissonance? *Journal of Management Studies, 39*(4), 419–436.

Gladwell, M. (2008). *Outliers: The story of success.* New York: Little, Brown.

Glickman, C. D. (1991). Pretending not to know what we know. *Educational Leadership, 48*(8), 4–10.

Goddard, R. (2001). Collective efficacy: A neglected construct in the study of schools and student achievement. *Journal of Educational Psychology, 93*(3), 467–476.

Goddard, R. D., Hoy, W. K., & Woolfolk, A. (2000). Collective teacher efficacy: Its meaning, measure, and effect on student achievement. *American Education Research Journal, 37*(2), 479–507.

Goleman, D. (1995). *Emotional intelligence: Why it can matter more than IQ.* New York: Bantam.

Goleman, D. (2006). *Social intelligence: The revolutionary new science of human relations.* New York: Bantam Dell.

Good, T. & McCaslin, M. (2008). *What we learned about research on school reform: Considerations for practice and policy.* Retrieved from http://www.tcrecord.org/Content.asp?contentid=15286.

Gordon, D. T. (2002). Fuel for reform: The importance of trust in changing schools. *Harvard Education Letter, 18*(4), 1–4.

Graham, P. (2007, January 22). The role of conversation, contention, and commitment in a professional learning community. Retrieved from http://cnx.org/content/m14270/1.1/.

Grinder, M. (1996). *ENVoY: A personal guide to classroom management.* Battle Ground, WA: Michael Grinder & Associates.

Grinder, M. (2007). *The elusive obvious: The science of non-verbal communication.* Battle Ground, WA: Michael Grinder & Associates.

Hargreaves, A., & Shirley, D. (2011). *The fourth way: The inspiring future for educational change.* Thousand Oaks, CA: Corwin.

Heath, C., & Heath, D. (2010). *Switch: how to change things when change is hard.* New York: Broadway Books.

Hock, D. (2000). *The birth of the chaordic age.* San Francisco: Berrett-Koehler.

Hoy, W. K., Tarter, C. J., & Hoy, A. W. (2006). Academic optimism of schools: A force for student achievement. *American Educational Research Journal, 43*(3), 425–446.

Hyerle, D. (2000). *A field guide to using visual tools.* Arlington, VA: Association for Supervision and Curriculum Development.

Isaacs, W. (1999). *Dialogue and the art of thinking together: A pioneering approach to communicating in business and in life.* New York: Random House.

Johnson, B. (1996). *Polarity management: Identifying and managing unsolvable problems.* Amherst, MA: HRD Press.

Joyce, B. (2004). How are professional learning communities created? History has a few messages. *Phi Delta Kappan, 86*(1), 76–83.

Klein, G. (1999). *Sources of power: How people make decisions.* Cambridge, MA: MIT Press.

Kohn, A. (1993). *Punished by rewards: The trouble with gold stars, incentive plans, A's, praise and other bribes.* Boston: Houghton Mifflin.

Kruse, S., & Louis, K. S. (2009). *Building strong school cultures: A guide to leading change.* Thousand Oaks, CA: Corwin.

Lankton, S., & Lankton, C. (1983). *The answer within: A clinical framework of Ericksonian hypnotherapy.* New York: Brunner/Masek.

Lipton, L., Wellman, B., & Humbard, C. (2003). *Mentoring matters: A practical guide to learning-focused relationships.* Arlington, MA: MiraVia.

Loden, M. (1985). *Feminine leadership.* New York: Crown Books.

Losada, M., & Heaphy, E. (2004). The role of positivity and connectivity in performance of business teams: A nonlinear dynamic model. *American Behavioral Scientist, 47*(6), 740–765.

Louis, K. S., Marks, H., & Kruse, S. (1996). Teachers' professional community in restructuring schools. *American Educational Research Journal, 33*(4), 757–798.

Malone, T. W. (2006, October 13). Transcript of remarks at the launch of the MIT Center for Collective Intelligence. Retrieved from http://cci.mit.edu/about/MaloneLaunchRemarks.html.

Marshall, J. (2010, September 30). How to measure the wisdom of a crowd. *Discovery News.* Retrieved from http://news.discovery.com/human/group-intelligence-wisdom-crowd.html.

Martin, M. (2006, December 21). Survey questionnaire construction (Research report series: Survey methodology #2006–13). Washington, DC: U.S. Census Bureau.

Maturana, H., & Varela, F. (1987). *The tree of knowledge: A new look at the biological roots of human understanding.* Boston: Shambhala Publications.

McLaughlin, M. (1990). The RAND change agent study revisited: Macro perspectives and micro realities. *Educational Researcher, 19*(9), 11–16.

McKanders, C. (2009). Appendix M: Using conflict as a resource. In R. J. Garmston & B. Wellman, *The adaptive school: A sourcebook for developing collaborative groups.* Norwood, MA: Christopher-Gordon.

Medina, J. (2008). *Brain rules: 12 principles for surviving and thriving at work, home, and school.* Seattle, WA: Pear Press.

Mehrabian, A. (2007). *Nonverbal communication.* Piscataway, NJ: Transaction.

Miller, G. (1963). The magical number seven, plus or minus two: Some limits in capacity for processing information. *Psychological Review, 63,* 81–97.

National Commission on Teaching and America's Future. (2003). *No dream denied: A pledge to America's children.* Washington, DC: Author.

National Commission on Teaching and America's Future. (2010). *Team up for the 21st century: What research and practice reveal about professional learning.* Washington, DC: Author.

Page, S. (2007). *The difference: How the power of diversity creates better groups, firms, schools, and societies.* Princeton, NJ: Princeton University Press.

Pfeffer, J. (2005). Changing mental models: HR's most important task. *Human Resource Management, 44*(2), pp. 123–128.

Pink, D. (2011). *Drive: The surprising truth about what motivates us.* New York: Riverhead Trade.

Poole, M. G., & O'Keafor, K. R. (1989). The effects of teacher efficacy and interactions among educators on curriculum implementation. *Journal of Curriculum and Supervision, 4*(2), 146–161.

Powell, B., & Powell, O. K. (2010). *Becoming an emotionally intelligent teacher.* Thousand Oaks, CA: Corwin.

Rock, D. (2009). *Your brain at work: Strategies for overcoming distraction, regaining focus and working smarter all day long.* New York: HarperBusiness.

Rokeach, M. (1964). *The three Christs of Ypsilanti.* New York: Vintage.

Rosenholtz, S. (1989). *Teacher's workplace: The social organization of schools.* New York: Longman.

Rowe, M. B. (1974). Relation of wait-time and rewards to the development of language, logic and fate control: Part II–Rewards. *Journal of Research in Science Teaching, 11,* 291–308.

Rowe, M. B. (1983). Getting chemistry off the killer course list. *Journal of Chemical Education, 60*(11), 954.

Rowe, M. B. (1986). Wait time: Slowing down may be a way of speeding up. *Journal of Teacher Education. 37*(1), 50.

Rugg, D. (1941). Experiments in wording questions: II. *Public Opinion Quarterly, 5*(1), 91–92.

Sanford, C. (1995). *Myths of organizational effectiveness at work.* Battle Ground, WA: Springhill Publications.

Saphier, J., Bigda-Peyton, T., & Pierson, G. (1989). *How to make decisions that stay made.* Alexandria, VA: Association for Supervision and Curriculum Development.

Schwarz, R. M. (2002). *The skilled facilitator: Practical wisdom for developing effective groups* (2nd ed.). San Francisco: Jossey-Bass.

Seeley, T. (2010). *Honeybee democracy.* Princeton, NJ: Princeton University Press.

Seligman, M. E. (1993). *What you can change and what you can't.* New York: Fawcett.

Sergiovanni, T. (1994). *Building community in schools.* San Francisco: Jossey-Bass.

Showers, B., & Joyce, B. (1996). The evolution of peer coaching. *Educational Leadership, 53*(6) 12–16.

Simon, H. A. (1982). *Models of bounded rationality: Empirically grounded economic reason, Vol. 3.* Cambridge, MA: MIT Press.

Sternberg, R. J., & Horvath, J. A. (1995). A prototype view of expert teaching. *Educational Researcher, 24*(6), 9–17.

Supovitz, J., & Christman, J. B. (2003, November). Developing communities of instructional practice: Lessons from

Cincinnati and Philadelphia. (CPRE Policy Brief, RB- 39). Philadelphia, PA: Consortium for Policy Research in Education.

Surowiecki, J. (2005). *The wisdom of crowds.* New York: Anchor Books.

Syed, M. (2010). *Bounce: Mozart, Federer, Picasso, Beckman and the science of success.* New York: HarperCollins.

Tapscott, D. & Williams, A.D. (2008). *Wikinomics: How mass collaboration changes everything.* New York: Penguin.

Taylor, S. E., Klein, L. C., Lewis, B. P., Gruenewald, T. L., Gurung, R. A., & Updegraff, J. A. (2000). Biobehavioral responses to stress in females: Tend-and-befriend, not fight-or-flight. *Psychological Review, 107*(3), 411–429.

Tschannen-Moran, M. (2004). *Trust matters: Leadership for successful schools.* San Francisco: Jossey-Bass.

Verdoux, P. (2011, January 19). Group intelligence, enhancement, and extended minds. Retrieved from http://ieet.org/index.php/IEET/more/4525.

Von Hippel, E. (2005). *Democratizing innovation.* Cambridge, MA: MIT Press.

Waldrop, M. M. (1992). *Complexity: The emerging science at the edge of order and chaos.* New York: Simon & Schuster.

Wellman, B. & Lipton, L. (2004). *Data-driven dialogue: A facilitator's guide to collaborative inquiry.* Arlington, MA: MiraVia.

Wheatley, M. J. (1992). *Leadership and the new science: Learning about organizations from an orderly universe.* San Francisco: Berrett-Koehler.

Wheatley, M. J. (2006). *Leadership and the new sciences: Discovering order in a chaotic world.* San Francisco, CA: Berrett-Koehler.

Woolley, A. W., Chabris, C. F., Pentland, A., Hashmi, M., & Malone, T. W. (2010). Evidence for a collective intelligence factor in the performance of human groups. *Science, 330*(6004), 686–688.

Wuchty, S., Jones, B., & Uzzi, B. (2007a). The increasing dominance of teams in the production of knowledge. *Science, 316*(5827), 1036-1039.

Wuchty, S., Jones, B., & Uzzi, B. (2007b). Science commentary: Why do team-authored papers get cited more? *Science, 317*(5844), 1496-1498.

Yoram, J., Crook, C., & Gunther, R. (2005). *The power of impossible thinking: Transform the business of your life and the life of your business.* Upper Saddle River, NJ: Wharton School Publishing.

Zimmerman, D. (1995). The linguistics of leadership. In L. Lambert (Ed.), *The constructivist leader* (pp. 104–120). New York: Teachers College Press.

Zoller, K., & Landry, C. (2010). *The choreography of presenting: The 7 essential abilities of effective presenters.* Thousand Oaks, CA: Corwin.

Index

Practice:
 expertise as matter of, 8
 facilitation as taking, 8–9
 trusting behaviors, 9–10
Praise, 126
Prefrontal cortex, 30
Presuming positive intentions:
 collaborative norm of, 88–89
 paraphrasing framed by, 88
 self-modification of, 130
Problems:
 mediational questions related to
   polarities of, 116–117
 polarities of, 112
 Polarity Map tool to map
   paradoxes or, 112–115
Processes:
 communicating decision-making,
   37–39
 definition of, 18, 161
 distinction between content and,
   18
 facilitator explanation of, 181
 group intelligence dependent on
   group, 68
 meeting standard on using only
   one at a time, 18–19
 monitoring internal meeting,
   28–29
 well-constructed agenda's
   description of, 61
Processing questions, 127
Processionary caterpillars study,
   73–74
Professional culture:
 emergence of school, 16
 how teacher talk can transform,
   89
 of inquiry versus isolation, 49
Pronouns, 171
Props:
 flip charts, 195–197, 198
   (figure)
 interactive white boards,
   197–198 (figure)
Providing data:
 as collaboration data, 87–88

of qualitative and quantitative
   data, 87
 self-modification through, 130
 See also Information
Providing protocols, 180–181

Quartet interactions, 59
Questions:
 to ask about decision-making
   topics, 41
 cross-categorical, 167–168
 focusing, 145–146
 invitational, 165
 learning to ask, 164–166
 mediational, 115–117, 166
 mediative power connected to
   focus of, 165–166
 Meeting Inventory
   Questionnaire, 127–129
 "miracle question," 109
 posing, 85–86, 130
 processing, 127
 scaffolding used to formulate
   effective, 167
 to ask when deciding to
   intervene, 184–185
 word banks used to formulate,
   167–168
 See also Communication;
   Inquiring skills; Language
   of facilitation

Ravlin, M., 215–221
The recorder:
 meeting role of, 31–32
 meeting tasks of, 32
 purposeful neutrality of, 31
Redirecting conversation, 186
Reference structures:
 energy sources linking deep and
   surface, 99
 examples of negative and
   positive surface, 100–101
 "primitive" experiences of, 97
Reflection:
 facilitation development
   through, 9

CORWIN
A SAGE Company

The Corwin logo—a raven striding across an open book—represents the union of courage and learning. Corwin is committed to improving education for all learners by publishing books and other professional development resources for those serving the field of PreK–12 education. By providing practical, hands-on materials, Corwin continues to carry out the promise of its motto: **"Helping Educators Do Their Work Better."**